MULTILEVEL MATH FUN

Instant Games & Activities for the Multilevel Classroom

Written by
Dr. Carl Seltzer

Editor: Teri L. Fisch
Illustrator: Darcy Tom
Cover Illustrator: Rick Grayson
Designer: Moonhee Pak
Cover Designer: Moonhee Pak
Art Director: Tom Cochrane
Project Director: Carolea Williams

© 2002 Creative Teaching Press, Inc., Huntington Beach, CA 92649
Reproduction of activities in any manner for use in the classroom and not for commercial sale is permissible.
Reproduction of these materials for an entire school or for a school system is strictly prohibited.

Table of Contents

Introduction 3
    Getting Started 4
    Organizing the Materials 5

NCTM Standards Correlation 6

Math Fun for the Whole Class
    Flash Card Activities 7
        Sequence the Numbers 8
        Addends to Sums 8
        Number Sentence Challenge 9
        How Many Objects? 9
        Create the Number 10
        Even and Odd Rules 10
        Baseball Math 11
        Calendar Math 12

Math Fun for Individuals
    By Numbers 13
    Find It 18
    Three for Sums 23
    A-Mazing Math Mazes 28
    The Path 33

Math Fun for Two Players
    The In-Between Game 38
    Tic-Fraction-Toe 43
    Watch for the Answer 48
    Earlier or Later? 52

Math Fun for Two or More Players
    Target the Number 54
    Use Your Memory 59
    Number Duel 64
    Score More 69
    Spin the Wheel 74

Manipulatives and Game Pieces
    Math Flash Cards 79
    Number Cards 84
    Fraction Cards 85
    Clocks 87
    Smile Squares 91
    Spinners 92

Answers 94

Introduction

Multilevel Math Fun 1–2 features games and activities designed to help children learn mathematical skills, problem-solving strategies, and critical thinking skills while having fun with math. Each game or activity includes directions and reproducibles for four different skill levels, with the least complex concepts first and the most complex last, which allows you to differentiate your math instruction to meet the needs of each child in your classroom. The math skills range from number recognition and counting to multidigit subtraction with regrouping to simple multiplication.

Choose from games and activities for the whole class, individuals, pairs, and small groups. Each game or activity begins with a teacher page that includes
- a short materials list with key math skills listed for each reproducible
- easy-to-follow directions for preparation and play
- helpful hints such as extension ideas and ways to foster student success

Use this information to introduce, set up, and implement each game or activity. Refer to the NCTM Standards Correlation chart (page 6) to identify the games and activities that focus on the specific skills and standards you want to target. This resource also features a variety of math manipulatives and game pieces and a handy answer key for the activities.

To extend learning, challenge children to modify the games or invent similar ones. Encourage them to create games at an appropriate level and write clear directions and rules. You will be amazed at the children's creativity and they will feel a sense of excitement as well as accomplishment when they see their classmates playing games they created!

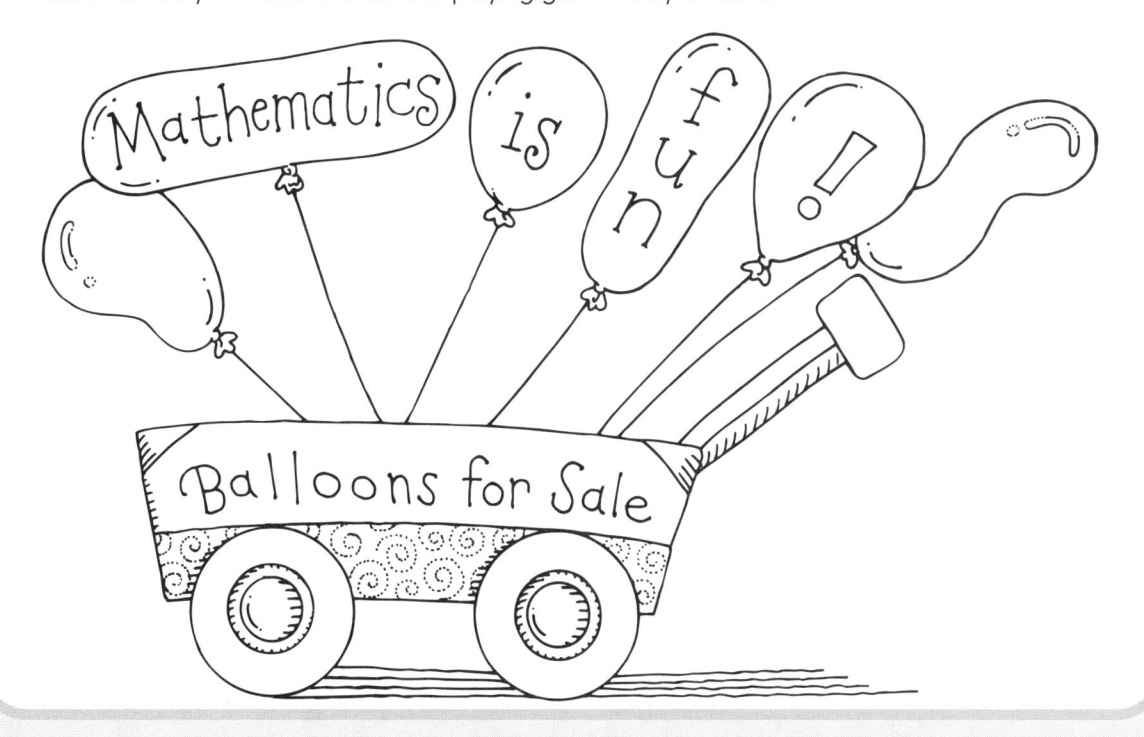

Getting Started

The math games and activities in this book provide a fun and easy way to differentiate curriculum. Model how to play each game before children begin to play. The following descriptions explain how to use the games and activities from each section in your classroom of multilevel learners.

Math Fun for the Whole Class

Begin with the activities in this section, which all use the Math Flash Cards (pages 79–83). The math concepts in these activities become progressively more difficult, but many of them can be adapted to meet your instructional needs. The activities will help you teach children how to use their set of flash cards to practice math skills at different levels. Use the activities in this section to help you assess the math "comfort level" of your whole class and individual children.

Math Fun for Individuals

Children do not have to complete the activities in this section in sequence, but they should have the necessary prerequisite skills before they start each activity. Review the directions for each activity, choose the skill level you wish to target, and select a reproducible at that level for every child to complete or for children who finish other work early to complete. Another option is to choose an activity and invite children to complete some or all of the reproducibles over a given period of time. Since the four reproducibles for each activity get progressively more difficult, children will complete them at different speeds and some children may not have the necessary skills to handle the more complex concepts yet. You may also choose to introduce an activity to the whole class and then have children complete one or more of the reproducibles for homework, as class work, at a center, or as a combination of these.

Math Fun for Two Players
Choose a different game each week, explain the general rules to the whole class, and provide time during the week for children to play it. Keep the game at a math center. Have children play it when they have finished another math assignment, or have the whole class play in pairs at the same time. With the second option, have the whole class play the same game, but each pair of children play at their own skill level. Assess children's math abilities by observing play at each level of the game. Once you feel a child has mastered one skill level, invite him or her to play the next level, and so on.

Math Fun for Two or More Players
Choose a different game each month, and teach the whole class or small groups of children how to play it. Then, have children play the game using the reproducible that addresses the math skill most appropriate to their skill level or the one that addresses the skills you want to target. Have groups of children play the game during center time, or divide the class into small groups and have the whole class play at the same time. Vary the reproducible children complete so that sometimes they start with the least complex concept (the first reproducible of a game) and at other times they start with the most complex one.

Organizing the Materials
Photocopy the reproducibles and game pieces on construction paper or card stock, and laminate them for durability. Have children use dry erase markers to write on the laminated materials so they can be used again and again. Place the materials for each game or activity in a large envelope or resealable plastic bag. Include a sheet that lists the name of the game or activity and a list of the materials. This makes it easy to keep track of the materials in each envelope or bag and you can quickly and easily hand them out to pairs or small groups of children. Encourage children to use manipulatives (e.g., linking cubes, poker chips) to keep score or to write tally marks on a piece of scratch paper.

NCTM Standards Correlation

The standards listed on the chart represent those identified by the National Council of Teachers of Mathematics. Use this chart to identify games and activities that address the standards you wish to reinforce.

	Addition	Addition with regrouping	Counting/Sequencing	Fractions	Multiplication	Number recognition/comparison	Subtraction	Subtraction with regrouping	Algebra	Geometry	Measurement	Problem solving
A-Mazing Math Mazes	X	X					X	X				
By Numbers	X	X	X				X	X				
Earlier or Later?											X	X
Find It			X			X				X		
Flash Card Activities	X	X	X		X	X	X	X			X	
The In-Between Game						X						X
Number Duel						X						
The Path	X	X					X	X	X			X
Score More	X				X		X					X
Spin the Wheel	X	X								X		X
Target the Number	X	X	X				X	X				
Three for Sums	X	X										
Tic-Fraction-Toe				X								X
Use Your Memory	X				X		X					
Watch for the Answer	X	X					X	X	X			X

Numbers & Operations covers: Addition, Addition with regrouping, Counting/Sequencing, Fractions, Multiplication, Number recognition/comparison, Subtraction, Subtraction with regrouping.

Flash Card Activities

Directions

1. Give each child a set of Math Flash Cards.

2. Have children cut apart the cards on the solid lines, fold them on the dotted lines, and tape or glue together each card so that the symbol and word are back-to-back.

3. Invite children to hole-punch their cards and place them on a metal ring.

4. Choose the appropriate activities (pages 8–12) for your class. Have children participate in the activities daily, weekly, or monthly, or use them as sponge activities.

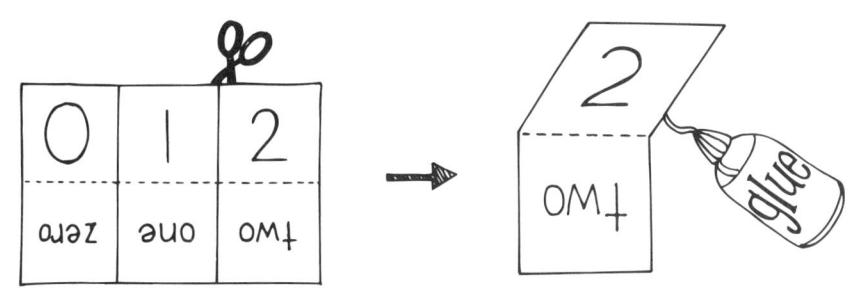

Cut apart the flash cards.

Fold each card on the dotted line and glue it together back-to-back.

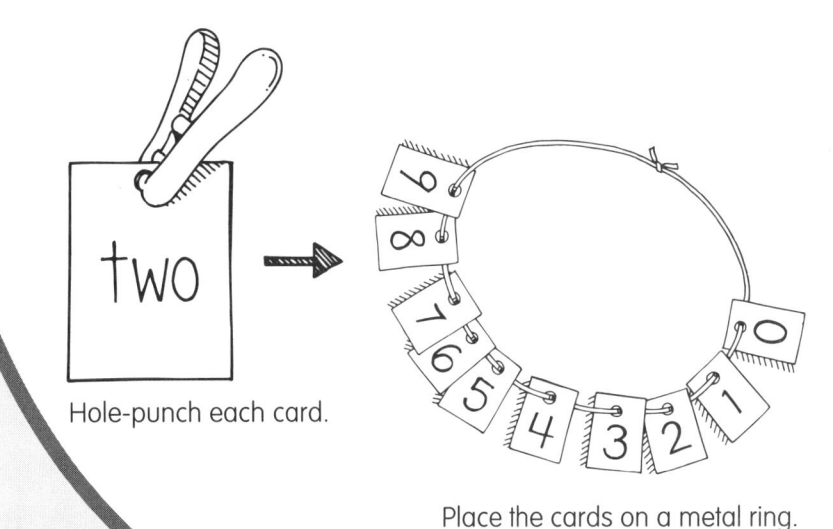

Hole-punch each card.

Place the cards on a metal ring.

Materials

- ✓ **Math Flash Cards** (pages 79–83)
- ✓ **scissors**
- ✓ **tape or glue**
- ✓ **hole punch**
- ✓ **metal rings**

Helpful Hints

- ➢ Photocopy the Math Flash Cards on card stock.
- ➢ Have children write their name or initials on each card.
- ➢ Use pipe cleaners twisted into rings instead of metal rings.

Math Fun for the Whole Class

> Flash Card Activities

Sequence the Numbers

Have a child stand at the front of the classroom and display a number card. Have a second child display the number card that continues the sequence of numbers and stand by the first child. Ask the class to determine if the correct card has been displayed. Continue to have volunteers determine the next number and display it, followed by the affirmation of the class. (Note: For numbers greater than 9, have two children combine their cards.) Extend the activity by having children use word cards and number cards, count by 2s (even and odd), or count backwards.

Materials

✓ **Math Flash Cards**
(pages 79–83)
SEQUENCING NUMBERS

Addends to Sums

Ask several children to randomly select a number card from their set of Math Flash Cards (duplicates are okay). Have each child stand at the front of the classroom. Invite the rest of the class to identify two or more cards that when added together
- have a sum of 5
- have a sum of 10
- have a sum of 20
- have a sum of ____ (randomly select a number)

Record children's responses in number sentence form on the board (e.g., 3 + 5 = 8, 4 + 4 = 8, 1 + 1 + 6 = 8). Have children identify differences to build subtraction skills (e.g., 9 − 4 = 5, 3 − 2 = 1).

Materials

✓ **Math Flash Cards**
(pages 79–83)
ADDITION,
SUBTRACTION

$9 + 9 + 2 = 20$

8 Math Fun for the Whole Class

> Flash Card Activities

Number Sentence Challenge

Divide the class into small groups. Have children use their number or word cards and their plus, minus, and equals cards to form addition and subtraction sentences. (Note: If the answer is greater than 10, have two children combine their cards.) Challenge groups to make the longest sentence, the shortest sentence, the sentence with the largest answer, and the sentence with the smallest answer. Invite groups to compare their sentences using greater than, less than, and equals cards.

Materials

✓ **Math Flash Cards**
(pages 79–83)
ADDITION,
SUBTRACTION,
NUMBER COMPARISON

How Many Objects?

Gather two sets of objects such as linking cubes and pencils. Have two children display the number cards that identify how many are in each set. Ask two other children to display the word cards that identify how many objects are in each set. Then, have several groups of children use their Math Flash Cards to show the fact families for the numbers in the two sets or equations that correspond to the numbers in the sets. For example, if you make a set of 9 linking cubes and a set of 2 pencils, the first children would display the number cards 9 and 2. The next children would display the word cards nine and two. Then, groups of children could show the equations $9 + 2 = 11$, $11 - 2 = 9$, $9 > 2$, $4 + 5 = 9$, and $10 - 8 = 2$.

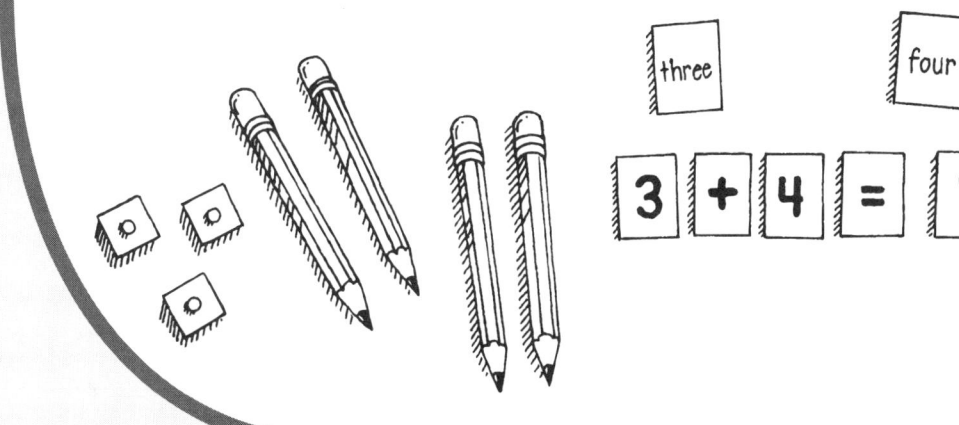

Materials

✓ **Math Flash Cards**
(pages 79–83)
COUNTING,
NUMBER/WORD/
OBJECT
CORRELATION,
ADDITION,
SUBTRACTION

✓ **2 sets of 0–9 objects**

Math Fun for the Whole Class

> Flash Card Activities

Create the Number

Divide the class into groups of three or four children. Ask each child to randomly choose a number card from his or her set of Math Flash Cards (duplicates are okay). Then, have the group use the selected number cards to form the following numbers:
- the least 3-digit number
- the number closest to 100 that they can make
- the number closest to the current calendar year that they can make
- the greatest even number possible
- the least odd number possible

Encourage groups to use their greater than, less than, and equals cards to compare each number with other groups' numbers.

Materials

✓ **Math Flash Cards**
(pages 79–83)
NUMBER COMPARISON

Even and Odd Rules

Gather two sets of Math Flash Cards. Ask two children to display two even numbers that each have one digit. Have them make an addition problem with the two numbers, record it on the board, and calculate the sum. Have several more volunteers create and solve problems with two even numbers. (Do not erase any of the problems.) Invite the class to look for a pattern. Guide children to see that the sum of two even numbers is always even. Repeat this activity using two odd numbers. Children should observe that two odd numbers always produce an even sum. Repeat this activity using an odd number and an even number. Children should observe that an odd number added to an even number always produces an odd sum. Challenge children to test the rules with two- and three-digit numbers.

Materials

✓ **Math Flash Cards**
(pages 79–83)
ADDITION

10 Math Fun for the Whole Class

Flash Card Activities

Baseball Math

Materials

- ✔ **Math Flash Cards**
  (pages 79–83)
  ADDITION, SUBTRACTION, REGROUPING, MULTIPLICATION
- ✔ **scratch paper**
- ✔ **timer or stopwatch**

Divide the class into two teams. Invite each team to write on separate pieces of paper a specified number of math problems for the other team to solve. (You may want to have them start with 20 or 30 problems.) Encourage teams to write three- and four-digit addition and subtraction problems or simple multiplication problems (e.g., 2 x 3 = ___, 5 x 1 = ___). Draw on the board a baseball diamond with a home plate, first base, second base, and third base. Draw a player or an "x" on home plate to show where the first batter is. Collect the teams' math problems, randomly select one problem (written by the second team) for the first team, and write it on the board. Hand out scratch paper, and challenge the whole team that is "at bat" or one player from that team to solve the problem in a specified amount of time (30 seconds or 1 minute) and display the answer using their Math Flash Cards. If the team displays the correct answer in the specified amount of time, their "player" moves to first base. Each correct answer moves a player to the next base. When a player gets a "run" by reaching home plate, the team scores a point. If the team displays an incorrect answer or does not display an answer in the specified amount of time, they receive an "out." This team continues to play until they have one or two outs (teacher discretion). Then, the other team goes up to "bat." Due to time constraints, you may wish to limit the number of "innings" in the game or you may want to play one inning of baseball each day.

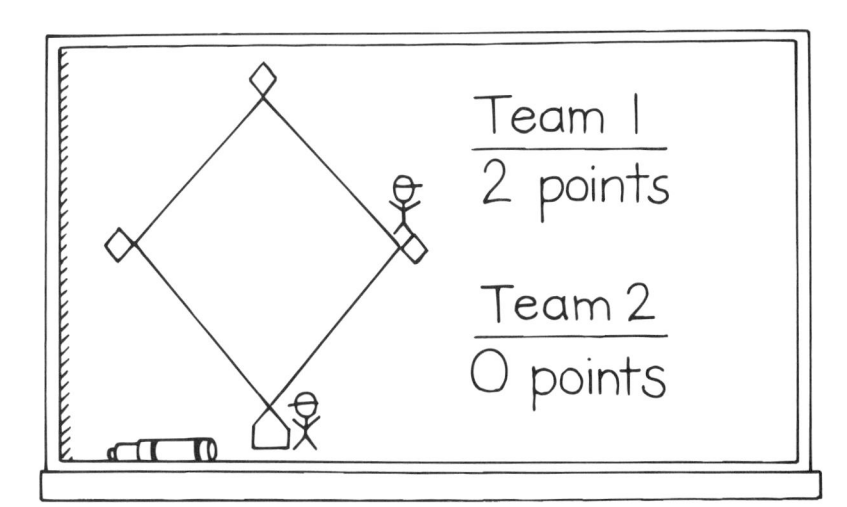

Math Fun for the Whole Class

Flash Card Activities

Calendar Math

Materials

- ✓ **Math Flash Cards**
  (pages 79–83)
  ADDITION, SUBTRACTION, REGROUPING, MULTIPLICATION
- ✓ **12-month calendars**
- ✓ **scratch paper**
- ✓ **small prizes**
  (e.g., pencils, bookmarks, erasers)

Invite children to work in groups of three. Have each group choose a name for their team. Record each name on the board. Give each group a 12-month calendar or a photocopy of a month from a calendar. Have groups solve a series of mathematical computation problems about the calendar. Tell children that the first team to work together to correctly display the answer with their Math Flash Cards will receive a point. Give a small prize to the team with the most points at the end of the activity. Use the following list of problems for the month of February as a guide:

- Add together all the Tuesday dates in the month of February. What is the sum?
- Add together all the dates in February. What is the sum?
- Add together the dates in the second week of February. What is the sum?
- Add together the date of Valentine's Day, Abraham Lincoln's birthday, and George Washington's birthday. What is the sum?
- Subtract the date of the first Saturday in February from the date of the last Saturday. What is the difference?
- Subtract the date of Groundhog Day from the date of Presidents' Day. What is the difference?
- Subtract the date of Wednesday in week 2 from the date of Friday in week 3. What is the difference?
- Multiply the first date of the month by the last date of the month. What is the product?

12 Math Fun for the Whole Class

By Numbers

Materials

Levels

- **1** — Connect the Numbers (page 14)
  COUNTING
- **2** — Dot Pictures (page 15)
  SKIP COUNTING
- **3** — Color the Sums (page 16)
  ADDITION, REGROUPING
- **4** — Color the Differences (page 17)
  SUBTRACTION, REGROUPING

✓ reproducibles (choose the appropriate level)

✓ crayons or colored pencils

Directions

1. Give each child a reproducible at the appropriate level and crayons or colored pencils.
2. Invite children to complete the activity by following the directions at the top of their paper.
3. Have children color their completed reproducible.

Helpful Hints

- Set copies of all four reproducibles on a table, and have children complete as many of them as they can during a class period. (Check children's work prior to their moving on to the next reproducible.)
- Invite children who have finished all the reproducibles to create their own connect-the-numbers picture or color-by-number picture. Have children complete each other's pictures.

Math Fun for Individuals

Name_____   Date_____

Connect the Numbers

Directions

Connect the numbers. Start at the number 1 and end at the number 20.

9•   •10   •11   •12   •13

•15
•14

8•

•16

7•

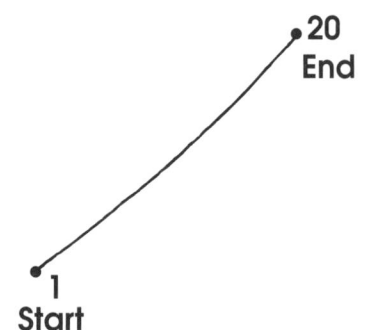

•17
•18

5•   6•_____•19

•20
End

4•   3•   2•   1•
Start

I counted by _____.

The picture is a _____.

Name_____ Date_____

Dot Pictures

Directions

Connect the numbers.

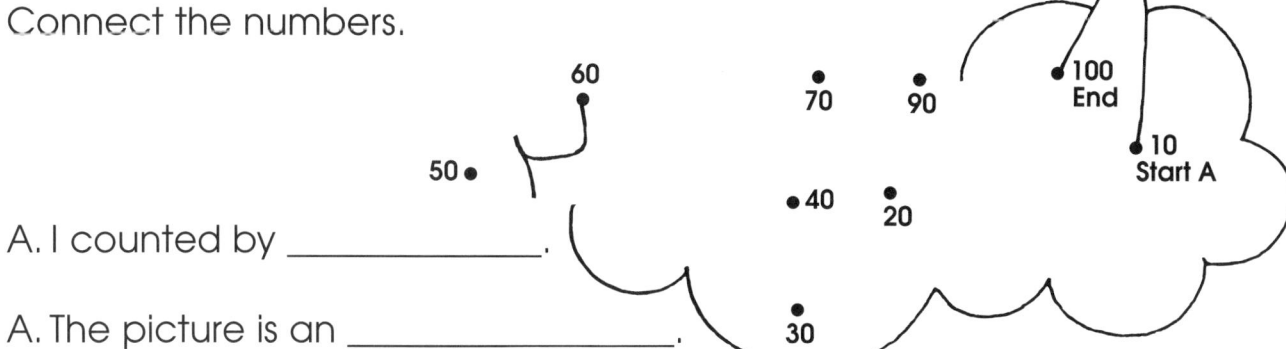

A. I counted by _____.

A. The picture is an _____.

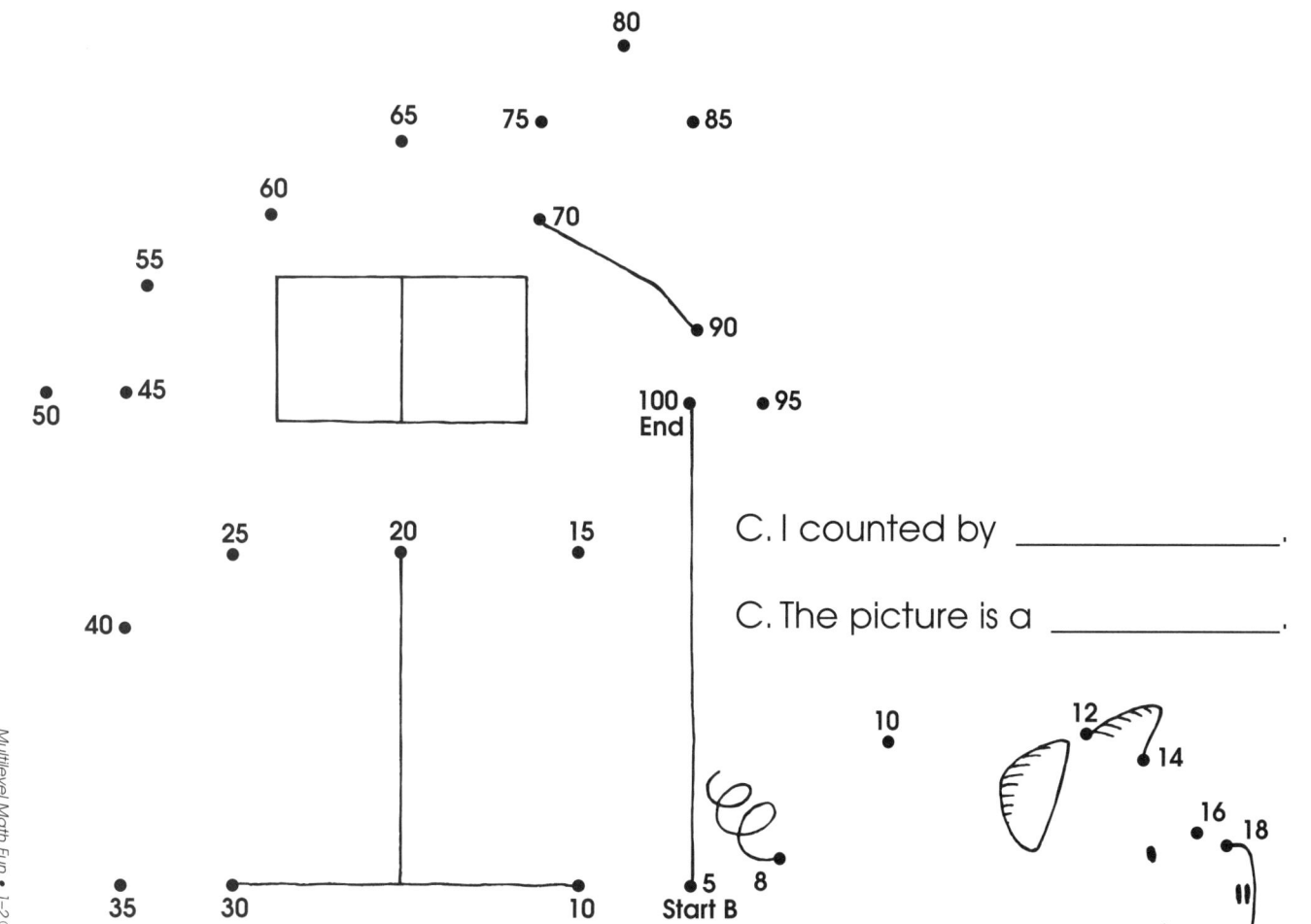

B. I counted by _____.

B. The picture is a _____.

C. I counted by _____.

C. The picture is a _____.

Math Fun for Individuals 15

Name_____ Date _____

Color the Sums

Directions

Complete the addition problems. Use the key to color each sum.

Key
40–black
75–purple
89–orange
92–brown
100–yellow
110–green
114–gray
120–blue
143–red

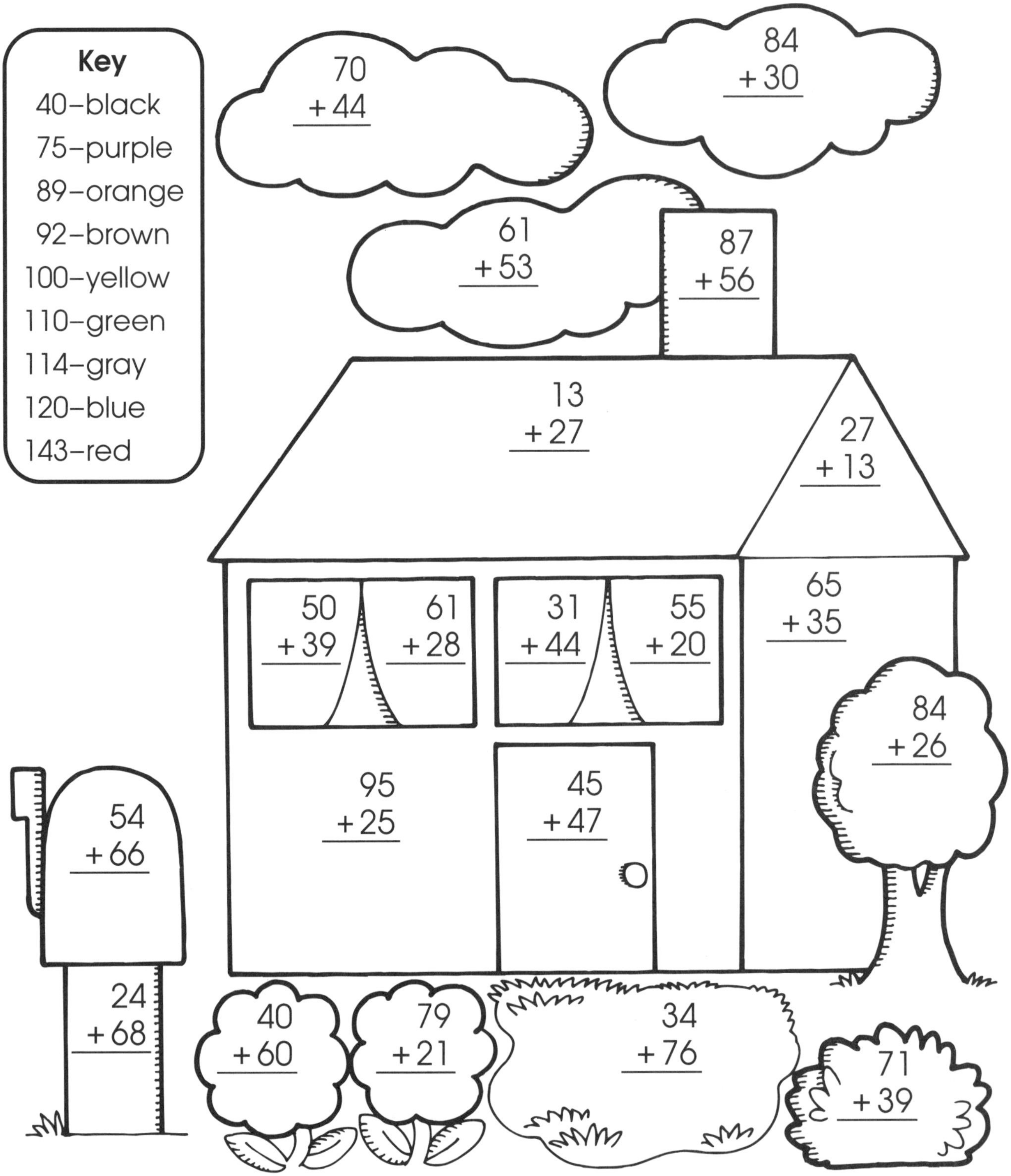

70 + 44

84 + 30

61 + 53

87 + 56

13 + 27

27 + 13

50 + 39

61 + 28

31 + 44

55 + 20

65 + 35

84 + 26

95 + 25

45 + 47

54 + 66

24 + 68

40 + 60

79 + 21

34 + 76

71 + 39

16 Math Fun for Individuals

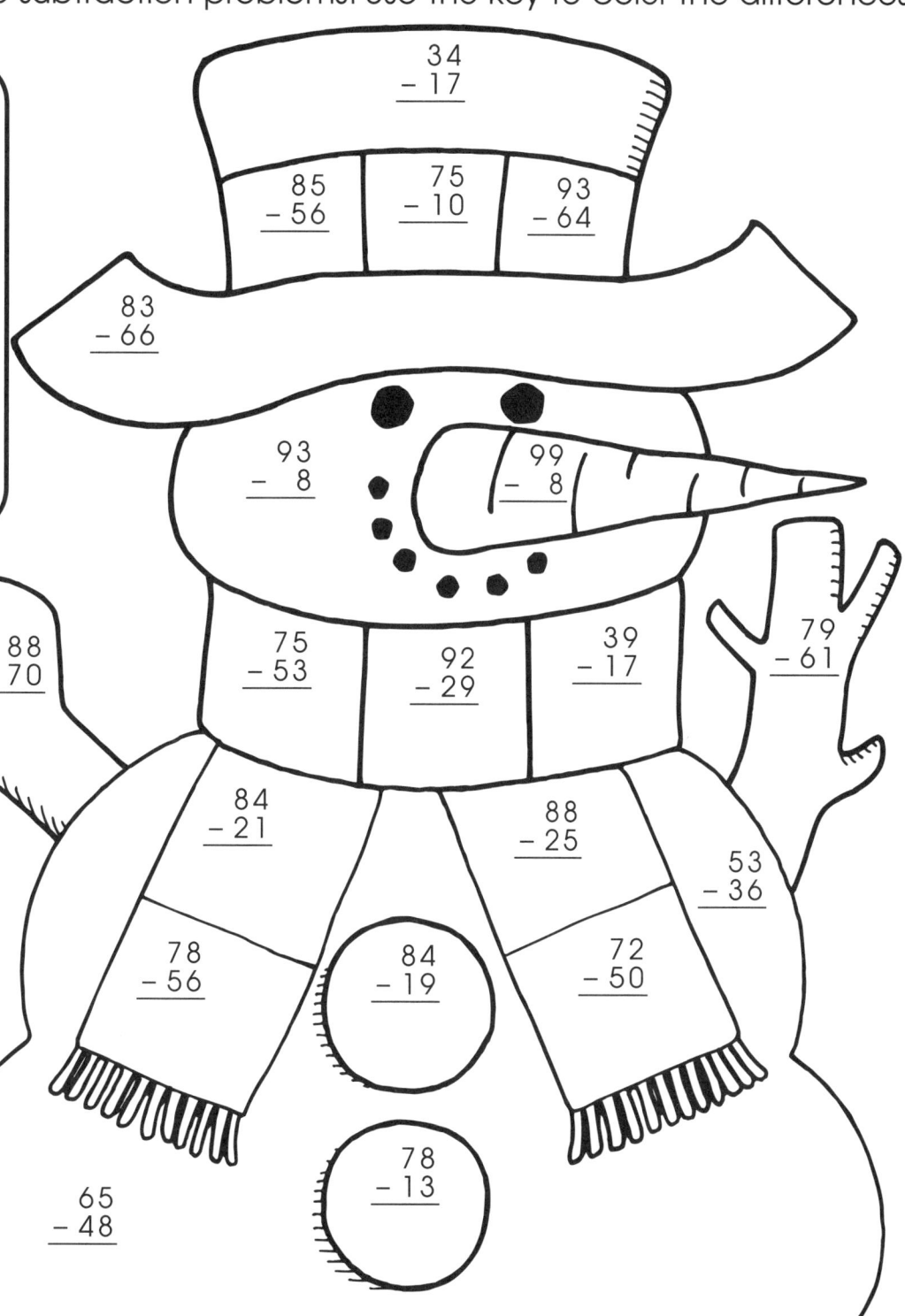

Name _____ Date _____

Color the Differences

Directions

Complete the subtraction problems. Use the key to color the differences.

Key
17—yellow
18—brown
22—purple
29—green
63—red
65—blue
85—white
91—orange

34 − 17

85 − 56
75 − 10
93 − 64

83 − 66

93 − 8
99 − 8

88 − 70
75 − 53
92 − 29
39 − 17
79 − 61

84 − 21
88 − 25
53 − 36

78 − 56
84 − 19
72 − 50

78 − 13

65 − 48

Math Fun for Individuals 17

Find It

Materials

Levels

1. ● Hidden Numbers (page 19)
   NUMBER RECOGNITION, COUNTING
2. ● Flat Shape Find (page 20)
   FLAT SHAPE RECOGNITION, COUNTING
3. ● Find the Solid Shapes (page 21)
   SOLID SHAPE RECOGNITION, COUNTING
4. ● Operations, Where Are You? (page 22)
   OPERATION SYMBOL RECOGNITION, COUNTING

✓ reproducibles (choose the appropriate level)

✓ 5 different colored pencils (for each child)

Directions

1. Give each child a reproducible at the appropriate level and a set of colored pencils.
2. Ask children to use a different colored pencil to trace each object and word in the key.
3. Invite children to find the objects hidden in the picture and color them according to their key.
4. Tell children to count each object and complete the sentences at the bottom of their paper.

Helpful Hints

- Give children flat shape (e.g., circle, oval) and solid shape (e.g., sphere, cylinder) manipulatives to help them recognize the hidden objects on pages 20 and 21.
- Challenge children to draw their own pictures containing hidden math objects and invite their classmates to find them.

18 Math Fun for Individuals

Name_____ Date_____

Hidden Numbers

Directions

Find the hidden numbers. Color them.

Key

0 zero
3 three
5 five
8 eight
9 nine

I found _____ hidden zeros.

I found _____ hidden threes.

I found _____ hidden fives.

I found _____ hidden eights.

I found _____ hidden nines.

Math Fun for Individuals 19

Name_____ Date_____

Flat Shape Find

Directions

Find the hidden shapes. Color them.

Key	
△	triangle
⬡	hexagon
☐	square
○	circle
▭	rectangle

A ▭ is called a _____. I found ____ of them.

A ☐ is called a _____. I found ____ of them.

A ○ is called a _____. I found ____ of them.

A ⬡ is called a _____. I found ____ of them.

A △ is called a _____. I found ____ of them.

Name_____   Date_____

Find the Solid Shapes

Directions

Find the hidden solids. Color them.

Key
sphere
pyramid
cube
cylinder
cone

A ⬚ is called a _____. I found ____ of them.

A ⬚ is called a _____. I found ____ of them.

A ⬚ is called a _____. I found ____ of them.

A ⬚ is called a _____. I found ____ of them.

A ⬚ is called a _____. I found ____ of them.

Math Fun for Individuals 21

Name_____ Date _____

Operations, Where Are You?

Directions

Find the hidden operation symbols. Color them.

Key
+ plus
− minus
= equals
< less than
> greater than

A < is called a _____ sign. I found ____ of them.

A + is called a _____ sign. I found ____ of them.

A > is called a _____ sign. I found ____ of them.

An = is called an _____ sign. I found ____ of them.

A − is called a _____ sign. I found ____ of them.

22 Math Fun for Individuals

Three for Sums

Materials

Levels

✓ **reproducibles (choose the appropriate level)**
- **1** — Sums of 10 (page 24)
  ADDITION TO 10
- **2** — Sums of 12 (page 25)
  ADDITION TO 12
- **3** — Sums of 20 (page 26)
  ADDITION TO 20
- **4** — Sums of 50 (page 27)
  1- AND 2-DIGIT ADDITION TO 50, REGROUPING

Directions

1 Give each child a reproducible at the appropriate level.

2 Invite children to find three numbers in a row across, down, or on a diagonal (only across or down on Sums of 10 reproducible) that when added together equal the target sum for their paper.

3 Have children circle as many groups of three addends as they can find.

4 Tell children to complete the sentence at the bottom of their paper.

Helpful Hints

- Ask children to use several different colored crayons or pencils to circle the groups of addends.
- Invite children to use scratch paper or a calculator to compute sums of 50 on page 27.
- Have children make up their own "sums of" page so that any three numbers in a row across, down, or on a diagonal equal the sum chosen. Invite classmates to complete each other's papers.

Math Fun for Individuals **23**

Name_____   Date_____

Sums of 10

Directions

Find three numbers in a row <u>across</u> or <u>down</u> that add up to the sum of 10. Circle each set of three numbers.

7	9	6	1	4
6	1	3	4	3
(7	2	1)	7	3
8	4	4	2	2
6	1	3	1	5

I found _____ sums of 10.

Name _____   Date _____

Sums of 12

Directions

Find three numbers in a row <u>across</u>, <u>down</u>, or <u>on a diagonal</u> that add up to the sum of 12. Circle each set of three numbers.

5	4	6	5	7
3	6	5	4	2
(2	9	1)	8	3
6	8	6	1	5
3	7	2	3	9
3	4	3	7	3

I found _____ sums of 12.

Name_____   Date _____

Sums of 20

Directions

Find three numbers in a row across, down, or on a diagonal that add up to the sum of 20. Circle each set of three numbers.

5	7	5	2	3	9
3	5	6	9	9	4
5	5	10	2	8	6
4	1	9	3	7	10
7	6	7	2	9	4
7	6	5	5	4	9
8	4	8	6	6	8

I found _____ sums of 20.

Name_____   Date_____

Sums of 50

Directions

Find three numbers in a row <u>across</u>, <u>down</u>, or <u>on a diagonal</u> that add up to the sum of 50. Circle each set of three numbers.

22	16	36	23	21	16	30
5	15	21	16	15	29	10
10	14	13	19	23	25	10
15	5	36	17	31	35	25
26	35	18	19	18	17	33
19	10	5	26	19	15	17
32	4	5	14	15	17	9
22	9	19	25	24	14	16
19	6	29	11	3	28	15

I found _____ sums of 50.

Math Fun for Individuals **27**

A-Mazing Math Mazes

Materials

Levels

✓ **reproducibles (choose the appropriate level)**

1. Addition Math Maze (page 29)
   ADDITION
2. Subtraction Math Maze (page 30)
   SUBTRACTION
3. Start-to-End Math Maze (page 31)
   ADDITION, SUBTRACTION
4. Regrouping Math Maze (page 32)
   ADDITION, SUBTRACTION, REGROUPING

Directions

1. Give each child a reproducible at the appropriate level.

2. Tell children to follow the math maze from "Start" to "End" with their finger.

3. Have children begin at the word *Start* and solve the addition or subtraction problems as they go through the maze to the word *End*.

4. Invite children to write their final answer in the star burst at the end of the maze.

Helpful Hints

➤ Encourage children to compute each addition or subtraction problem along the maze path on scratch paper and then record their answer on the side of the maze.

➤ Invite children to check their final answer with a calculator.

➤ Use correction fluid to delete the numbers on the mazes. (Leave the operation symbols.) Laminate the reproducibles. Invite children to use dry erase markers to write numbers in the boxes and complete their maze.

28 Math Fun for Individuals

Addition Math Maze

Directions

Follow the math maze from "Start" to "End." Solve the addition problems as you go. Write the final sum in the star burst.

Start → 5 + 1 + 3 + 7 + 2 + 4 + 0 + 2 = ★

Name _____ Date _____

Subtraction Math Maze

Directions

Follow the math maze from "Start" to "End." Solve the subtraction problems as you go. Write the final difference in the star burst.

Start					
38	3	–	0		
–	–		–		
5	5		6	0	=
–	–		–	–	
2	4		7	2	
–	1	–		1	–

End

30 Math Fun for Individuals

Name_____ Date_____

Start-to-End Math Maze

Directions

Follow the math maze from "Start" to "End." Solve the addition and subtraction problems as you go. Write the final answer in the star burst.

−	5	+		−	6	+
6		1		4		3
+		−		−		+
4		3		4		7
−		−		−		−
3		1		8		6
+		+		+		+
2		2		6		3 =
+		+		+		
1		3	−	4		
Start						

Math Fun for Individuals 31

Name_____   Date_____

Regrouping Math Maze

Directions

Follow the math maze from "Start" to "End." Solve the addition and subtraction problems as you go. Write the final answer in the star burst.

−	13	+		+	12	−
2		16		13		46
+		+		−		−
6		9		7		4
−		−		−		+
8		18		41		12	= ✦
+		−		+		
24		10		34		
+		+		−		
13		17	+	11		
Start

End

The Path

Materials

Levels

1. ● Bird's Path to 10 (page 34)
   ADDITION, PROBLEM SOLVING, ALGEBRA
2. ● Spider's Path to 5 (page 35)
   SUBTRACTION, PROBLEM SOLVING, ALGEBRA
3. ● Monkey's Path to 40 (page 36)
   ADDITION, REGROUPING, PROBLEM SOLVING, ALGEBRA
4. ● Snail's Path to 15 (page 37)
   SUBTRACTION, REGROUPING, PROBLEM SOLVING, ALGEBRA

✔ reproducibles (choose the appropriate level)

✔ scratch paper

Directions

1. Give each child a reproducible at the appropriate level and a piece of scratch paper.

2. Have children identify the target number on their paper. Tell them to find a "path" of numbers they can use to create an addition or a subtraction sentence (depending on their reproducible) that equals their target number. Have them begin at the number below the word "Start" and connect a path of numbers by drawing a line or shading the boxes until they reach the number above the word "End." (Note: The path follows straight lines right, left, up, and down.) Encourage children to compute their answers on the scratch paper.

3. Have children complete the sentence at the bottom of their paper by writing a number sentence with the numbers along their path (e.g., 3 + 2 + 5 + 4 + 6 = 20).

Helpful Hints

➤ Tell children to lightly draw a line with their pencil along the paths they try until they find the correct one, and then have them darken it or shade the boxes. Or, laminate the reproducibles, and have children write on them with dry erase markers.

➤ Challenge children to race against other children or use a stopwatch to see who can correctly complete the path the fastest.

➤ Invite children to check their answers with a calculator.

Math Fun for Individuals

Name _____ Date _____

Bird's Path to 10

Directions

Help the bird fly to its nest. Begin at the number under "Start." Find the path of numbers that adds up to 10. End at the number above "End." Write an addition sentence with the numbers you added.

Start

7	6	2	3	2
3	6	5	4	1
2	3	0	8	9
4	0	1	1	0
3	2	4	9	2

End
10

The path of numbers that adds up to 10 is

_____.

34 Math Fun for Individuals

Name_____ Date _____

Spider's Path to 5

Directions

Help the spider crawl to its web. Begin at the number under "Start." Find the path of numbers that when subtracted equals 5. End at the number above "End." Write a subtraction sentence with the numbers you subtracted.

Start

20	10	5	18	16
9	9	7	3	2
4	6	1	0	6
8	3	4	2	3
5	4	2	1	2

End 5

The path of numbers that when subtracted equals 5 is

_____.

Math Fun for Individuals 35

Name_____ Date _____

Monkey's Path to 40

Directions

Help the monkey find its banana. Begin at the number under "Start." Find the path of numbers that adds up to 40. End at the number above "End." Write an addition sentence with the numbers you added.

Start

3	9	1	7	2	0	4	9
1	8	2	3	4	8	1	3
9	7	9	5	7	5	8	0
6	0	8	0	6	2	3	2
1	2	9	3	6	8	1	4
8	6	1	7	3	1	6	0
5	4	4	6	3	5	4	7
2	7	5	0	1	5	9	4

End 40

The path of numbers that adds up to 40 is

_____.

36 Math Fun for Individuals

Name_____   Date_____

Snail's Path to 15

Directions

Help the snail find its new shell. Begin at the number under "Start." Find the path of numbers that when subtracted equals 15. End at the number above "End." Write a subtraction sentence with the numbers you subtracted.

Start

51	16	49	15	68	74	89	38
15	22	9	13	4	5	6	3
6	9	8	1	0	2	10	1
8	2	7	9	1	4	0	3
10	4	0	7	2	10	9	7
0	6	1	6	4	3	6	2
5	7	8	3	2	0	1	8
3	1	0	8	2	3	7	1

End
15

The path of numbers that when subtracted equals 15 is

_____.

The In-Between Game

Materials

Levels

1. ● In-Between Ones (page 39)
   NUMBER COMPARISON OF ONES, PROBLEM SOLVING
2. ● In-Between Tens (page 40)
   NUMBER COMPARISON OF TENS, PROBLEM SOLVING
3. ● In-Between Hundreds (page 41)
   NUMBER COMPARISON OF HUNDREDS, PROBLEM SOLVING
4. ● In-Between Thousands (page 42)
   NUMBER COMPARISON OF THOUSANDS, PROBLEM SOLVING

✓ reproducibles (choose the appropriate level)
✓ **Number Cards** (page 84)
✓ construction paper
✓ resealable plastic bags (1 for each player)

Directions

1. Photocopy on construction paper one set of Number Cards for each player. Cut apart the cards, and store each set in a separate bag.

2. Give each pair of children a reproducible at the appropriate level and two bags of cards. Tell each child to shuffle his or her cards before each turn and place them facedown in a pile.

3. Have player 1 draw cards from his or her pile and place them faceup on the game board, in row A and then row C.

4. Tell player 2 to decide whether or not he or she wants to try to draw a number that will be sequentially "in between" the numbers in row A and row C. If he or she decides not to draw a number, no points are scored, the game board is cleared, and players alternate roles. If player 2 decides to draw a number, have him or her draw cards and place them faceup on the game board in row B.

5. Ask player 2 to read aloud the number in row B. If it is between the numbers in row A and row C, player 2 scores 5 points. If it is not between the numbers, player 1 scores 5 points. Have players alternate roles until a player scores 25 points.

Helpful Hints

➤ Give each player a set of Number Cards photocopied on different colors of paper.

➤ Explain to children that it does not matter if row A or row C has the higher number as long as the number in row B is between the two numbers.

38 Math Fun for Two Players

In-Between Ones

Directions

- Player 1: Draw 1 card. Put it in row A. Draw 1 more card. Put it in row C.

- Player 2: Do you think you can draw a number that will be in between the numbers in row A and row C?

  No: Clear the game board.

  Yes: Draw 1 card. Put it in row B. If your number is in between the numbers in row A and row C, you score 5 points. If your number is not in between, player 1 scores 5 points.

- Take turns. Play until a player has 25 points.

A.

ones

B.

ones

C.

ones

Math Fun for Two Players 39

In-Between Tens

Directions

- **Player 1**: Draw 2 cards. Put them in row A. Draw 2 more cards. Put them in row C.

- **Player 2**: Do you think you can draw a number that will be in between the numbers in row A and row C?

  <u>No</u>: Clear the game board.

  <u>Yes</u>: Draw 2 cards. Put them in row B. If your number is in between the numbers in row A and row C, you score 5 points. If your number is not in between, player 1 scores 5 points.

- Take turns. Play until a player has 25 points.

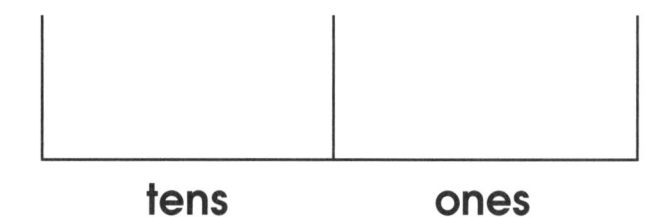

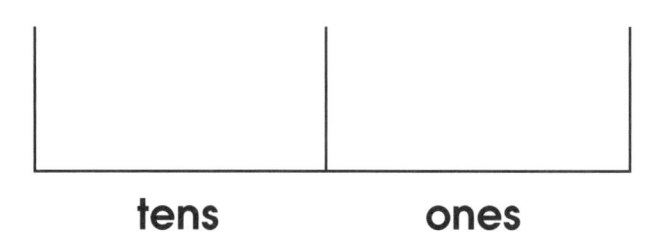

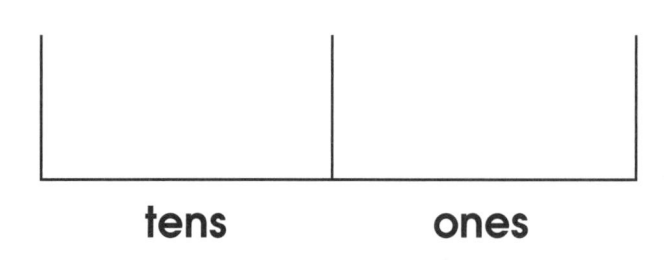

A.

tens	ones

B.

tens	ones

C.

tens	ones

40 Math Fun for Two Players

In-Between Hundreds

Directions

- Player 1: Draw 3 cards. Put them in row A. Draw 3 more cards. Put them in row C.

- Player 2: Do you think you can draw a number that will be in between the numbers in row A and row C?

  No: Clear the game board.

  Yes: Draw 3 cards. Put them in row B. If your number is in between the numbers in row A and row C, you score 5 points. If your number is not in between, player 1 scores 5 points.

- Take turns. Play until a player has 25 points.

A.

hundreds	tens	ones

B.

hundreds	tens	ones

C.

hundreds	tens	ones

In-Between Thousands

Directions

- Player 1: Draw 4 cards. Put them in row A. Draw 4 more cards. Put them in row C.

- Player 2: Do you think you can draw a number that will be in between the numbers in row A and row C?

  No: Clear the game board.

  Yes: Draw 4 cards. Put them in row B. If your number is in between the numbers in row A and row C, you score 5 points. If your number is not in between, player 1 scores 5 points.

- Take turns. Play until a player has 25 points.

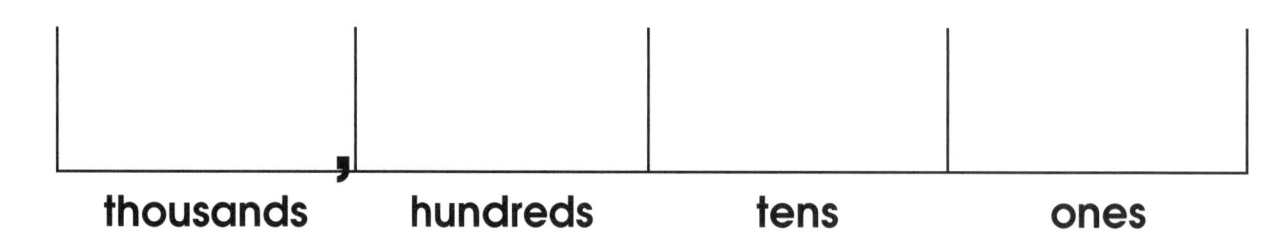

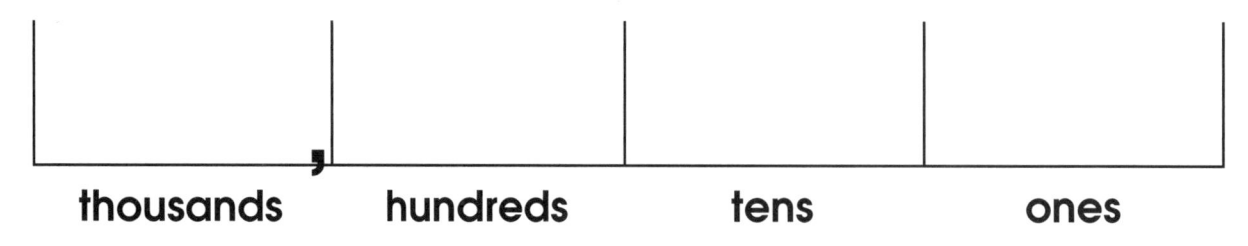

A.

| thousands | hundreds | tens | ones |

B.

| thousands | hundreds | tens | ones |

C.

| thousands | hundreds | tens | ones |

42 Math Fun for Two Players

Tic-Fraction-Toe

Materials

Levels

- ✔ **reproducibles** (choose the appropriate level)
  1. ● Bear Fraction Board (page 44)
     FRACTIONS: ONE WHOLE, ONE HALF, ONE THIRD, ONE QUARTER
  2. ● Toucan Fraction Board (page 45)
     FRACTIONS: WHOLES, HALVES, THIRDS, QUARTERS
  3. ● Snake Fraction Board (page 46)
     FRACTIONS: FIFTHS, SIXTHS, EIGHTHS, TENTHS, SIXTEENTHS
  4. ● Octopus Fraction Board (page 47)
     FRACTIONS: FIFTHS, SIXTHS, EIGHTHS, TENTHS, SIXTEENTHS
- ✔ **Fraction Cards** (pages 85–86)
- ✔ **construction paper** (2 colors for each pair)
- ✔ **resealable plastic bags** (1 for each child)

Directions

1. Make two photocopies of Fraction Cards Set A and Set B. Shade one page of Set A to match the fractions on the Bear Fraction Board and one page to match the fractions on the Toucan Fraction Board. Shade one page of Set B to match the fractions on the Snake Fraction Board and one page to match the fractions on the Octopus Fraction Board. Use these shaded reproducibles when making class sets.

2. For each pair of children, prepare two sets of the fraction cards (each on a different color of construction paper) that correspond to their fraction board reproducible. Cut apart the cards, put each set in a bag, and label it *Set A* or *Set B*. For example, photocopy the Fraction Cards Set A on red and blue paper for a pair of children with the Bear Fraction Board. Place each child's cards in a bag, and label it *Set A*.

3. Give each pair a fraction board reproducible and two bags of cards in two different colors. Tell each child to place the cards in a pile.

4. Tell players to take turns picking up one of their cards and placing it on the matching fraction on the game board. The first player to get three of his or her fraction pieces in a row across, down, or on a diagonal wins. If players cannot play the piece they picked, they lose that turn.

Helpful Hints

➢ Have children practice fraction recognition. Ask them to shade the Fraction Cards for homework or at a center.

➢ When children play with their fraction pieces facedown, the game provides randomness. When children play with their fraction pieces faceup, the game promotes problem-solving strategies. Have children switch how their pieces face.

Math Fun for Two Players

Bear Fraction Board

Directions

- Put your Set A Fraction Cards in a pile facedown.
- Take turns picking a card. Put your card on the matching fraction on the game board. The first player to get three cards in a row <u>across</u>, <u>down</u>, or <u>on a diagonal</u> wins. If you cannot play the card you picked, you lose your turn.

$\frac{1}{1}$	$\frac{1}{2}$	$\frac{1}{3}$
$\frac{1}{3}$	$\frac{1}{4}$	$\frac{1}{2}$
$\frac{1}{4}$	$\frac{1}{1}$	$\frac{1}{2}$

Toucan Fraction Board

Directions

- Put your Set A Fraction Cards faceup in rows.
- Take turns picking a card. Put your card on the matching fraction on the game board. The first player to get three cards in a row across, down, or on a diagonal wins. If you cannot play the card you picked, you lose your turn.

$\frac{1}{2}$	$\frac{2}{4}$	$\frac{2}{3}$
1	$\frac{1}{2}$	$\frac{2}{2}$
$\frac{3}{4}$	$\frac{1}{1}$	$\frac{1}{3}$

Snake Fraction Board

Directions

- Put your Set B Fraction Cards in a pile facedown.
- Take turns picking a card. Put your card on the matching fraction on the game board. The first player to get three cards in a row <u>across</u>, <u>down</u>, or <u>on a diagonal</u> wins. If you cannot play the card you picked, you lose your turn.

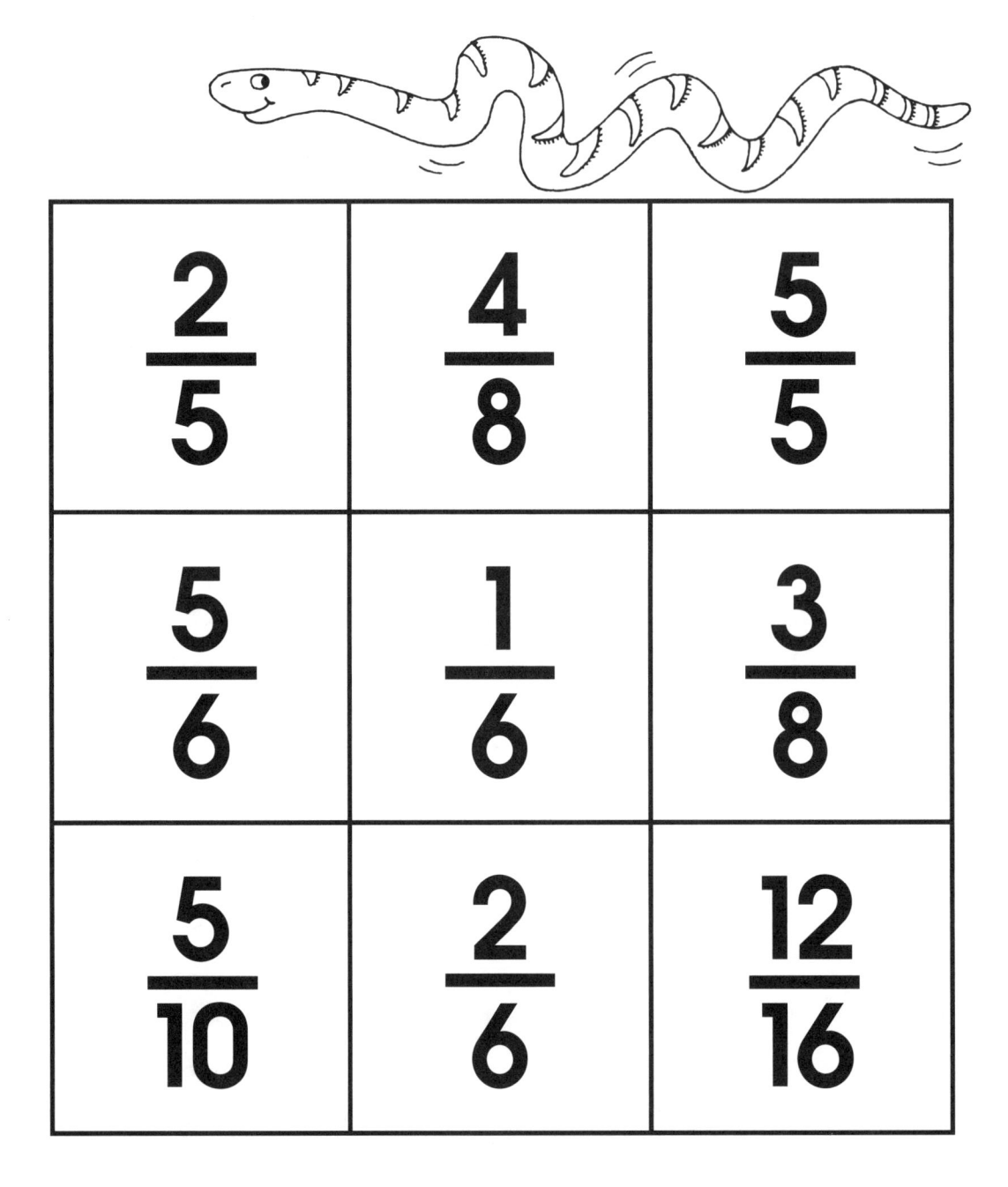

$\dfrac{2}{5}$	$\dfrac{4}{8}$	$\dfrac{5}{5}$
$\dfrac{5}{6}$	$\dfrac{1}{6}$	$\dfrac{3}{8}$
$\dfrac{5}{10}$	$\dfrac{2}{6}$	$\dfrac{12}{16}$

Octopus Fraction Board

Directions

- Put your Set B Fraction Cards faceup in rows.
- Take turns picking a card. Put your card on the matching fraction on the game board. The first player to get three cards in a row <u>across</u> or <u>down</u> (not on a diagonal) wins. If you cannot play the card you picked, you lose your turn.

$\frac{4}{6}$	$\frac{6}{8}$	$\frac{0}{5}$
$\frac{2}{6}$	1	$\frac{5}{10}$
$\frac{15}{16}$	$\frac{6}{6}$	$\frac{0}{8}$

Math Fun for Two Players 47

Watch for the Answer

Materials

- **Watch for the Answer Rules Sheets reproducible** (page 49)
  ADDITION, SUBTRACTION, REGROUPING, PROBLEM SOLVING, ALGEBRA
- **Three for the Answer reproducible** (page 50)
- **Four for the Answer reproducible** (page 51)
- **Number Cards** (page 84)
- **construction paper**
- **resealable plastic bags** (1 for each child)

Directions

1. Photocopy on construction paper the Watch for the Answer Rules Sheets reproducible, and cut it apart. Photocopy on construction paper a set of Number Cards for each child. Cut apart the cards, and store each set in a separate bag.

2. Give each pair of children a reproducible at the appropriate level, a game rules sheet, and two bags of cards.

3. Tell players to take turns placing a card anywhere on the game board. Explain that the object of the game is to create a straight row (across, down, or on a diagonal) of numbers that equals the target number by performing the operation on their rules sheet. Tell children that cards cannot be moved once they are placed.

4. The winner is the player who puts the last number in a row to make the row equal the target number. If no row equals the target number, the game is a tie and play starts over. Encourage children to play until a player has won five games.

Helpful Hints

- Photocopy the Number Cards on two different colors of construction paper so player 1 and player 2 have different colored pieces.
- Add challenge to the game at any level. Give player 1 a set of odd numbers and player 2 a set of even numbers. Or, tell players to achieve the target number only in a vertical, horizontal, or diagonal row, rather than any of the three.

48 Math Fun for Two Players

Watch for the Answer Rules Sheets

The Game of 15 Rules (Addition)
- Use Three for the Answer (page 50) to play.
- Try to make a straight row of three numbers that add up to 15.
- Take turns putting a card on the game board.
- The winner is the player who puts the third number in a row to make the numbers in the row add up to 15. If no row equals 15, the game is a tie.
- Play until a player wins five games.

The Game of 1 Rules (Subtraction)
- Use Three for the Answer (page 50) to play.
- Try to make a straight row of three numbers that when subtracted equal 1.
- Take turns putting a card on the game board.
- The winner is the player who puts the third number in a row to make the numbers in the row subtract to equal 1. If no row equals 1, the game is a tie.
- Play until a player wins five games.

The Game of 30 Rules (Addition with regrouping)
- Use Four for the Answer (page 51) to play.
- Try to make a straight row of four numbers that add up to 30.
- Take turns putting a card on the game board.
- The winner is the player who puts the fourth number in a row to make the numbers in the row add up to 30. If no row equals 30, the game is a tie.
- Play until a player wins five games.

The Game of 0 Rules (Subtraction with regrouping)
- Use Four for the Answer (page 51) to play.
- Try to make a straight row of four numbers that when subtracted equal 0.
- Take turns putting a card on the game board.
- The winner is the player who puts the fourth number in a row to make the numbers in the row subtract to equal 0. If no row equals 0, the game is a tie.
- Play until a player wins five games.

Three for the Answer

50 Math Fun for Two Players

Four for the Answer

Earlier or Later?

Materials

Levels

1. ● Hour Clocks (page 87)
   TELLING TIME TO THE HOUR
2. ● Half-Hour Clocks (page 88)
   TELLING TIME TO THE HALF HOUR
3. ● Quarter-Hour Clocks (page 89)
   TELLING TIME TO THE QUARTER HOUR
4. ● 5-Minute Clocks (page 90)
   TELLING TIME TO 5 MINUTES

✓ reproducibles (choose the appropriate level)

✓ **Earlier or Later? Game Board** (page 53)
   COMPARING TIME, PROBLEM SOLVING

✓ resealable plastic bags (1 for each pair)

Directions

1. Photocopy on construction paper sets of the clock reproducibles, cut them apart, and store each set of clocks in a separate labeled bag as follows: *Set A (Hour Clocks), Set B (Hour Clocks and Half-Hour Clocks), Set C (Hour Clocks, Half-Hour Clocks, and Quarter-Hour Clocks), Set D (Hour Clocks, Half-Hour Clocks, Quarter-Hour Clocks, and 5-Minute Clocks).*

2. Give each pair of children an Earlier or Later? Game Board and a bag of clock cards. Have a player shuffle the cards and put them facedown.

3. Have player 1 pick a clock card, place it faceup on the center box, and read aloud the time shown and what time of day it is.

4. Challenge player 2 to decide whether he or she will pick a clock with an earlier time or a later time. If the player chooses "earlier," he or she will pick a card and put it faceup in the top box. If the player chooses "later," he or she will pick a card and put it faceup in the bottom box.

5. If player 2 chose correctly, he or she scores 2 points. If player 2 chose incorrectly, player 1 scores 2 points. Have players alternate roles until a player scores 10 points.

Helpful Hints

➤ Photocopy each clock reproducible on a different color of paper to help with cleanup and organization.

➤ Review with the class that 12:00 a.m. is midnight and 12:00 p.m. is noon. Discuss that 12:00 p.m. is later than 6:00 a.m. and earlier than 6:00 p.m.

➤ Make two sets of each clock reproducible, and invite children to play Memory with the clock cards.

52 Math Fun for Two Players

Earlier or Later? Game Board

Directions

- Player 1: Pick a clock card. Put it faceup on the center box on the game board. Read aloud the time shown and what time of day it is.

- Player 2: Decide whether the clock card you will pick will show an earlier time or a later time than the card in the center box. If you think it will be "earlier," pick a clock card and put it faceup in the top box. If you think it will be "later," pick a clock card and put it faceup in the bottom box.

- If player 2 chose correctly, he or she scores two points. If player 2 chose incorrectly, player 1 scores two points.

- Play until a player scores 10 points.

Earlier

Time

Later

Math Fun for Two Players 53

Target the Number

Materials

Levels

1. ● Add to the Target (page 55)
   ADDITION
2. ● Subtract to Get the Target (page 56)
   SUBTRACTION
3. ● Get the Target (page 57)
   ADDITION, SUBTRACTION
4. ● Double-Digit Target (page 58)
   ADDITION, SUBTRACTION, REGROUPING

✓ reproducibles (choose the appropriate level)
✓ timers
✓ calculators

Directions

Helpful Hints

➤ On pages 55 and 56, encourage children to add or subtract more than two numbers in each equation (e.g., 1 + 4 + 2 = 7). On pages 57 and 58, encourage children to use addition and subtraction in each equation (e.g., 4 + 6 – 7 = 3).

➤ Photocopy reproducibles on colored paper. Collect the completed reproducibles, cut apart the boxes, and hole-punch them. Use yarn to connect the boxes for each target number to create a "quilt."

1. Divide the class into small groups. Give each group a timer, and give each child in a group the same reproducible and a calculator. Invite one child in each group to set the timer and say *Start* and *Stop*.

2. Have players focus only on the number in box A of their reproducible. (You can have them fold their paper to show only one box.)

3. Invite players to use the operation(s) listed to write in the box as many equations that equal the target number as they can in a specified amount of time (e.g., 2 minutes).

4. Tell players to count how many equations they wrote and record the number on their paper. Have them use a calculator to check their answers. Tell players to circle their correct equations, count them, and record the number on their paper. Then, have group members compare their papers to see who wrote the most correct equations.

5. Have players repeat the activity for boxes B, C, and D. The player with the most correct equations is the winner.

54 Math Fun for Two or More Players

Name_____ Date_____

Add to the Target

Directions

- Set the timer. Write in box A as many <u>addition</u> equations as you can that equal 7.
- Count how many equations you wrote. Write the number at the bottom of the paper. Check your answers with a calculator. Circle the correct answers and count them. Write the number at the bottom of the paper.
- Set the timer. Repeat the activity for the numbers in boxes B, C, and D.

A. **7**	B. **8**
C. **6**	D. **9**

A. I wrote _____ equations.
B. I wrote _____ equations.
C. I wrote _____ equations.
D. I wrote _____ equations.

A. I wrote _____ correct equations.
B. I wrote _____ correct equations.
C. I wrote _____ correct equations.
D. I wrote _____ correct equations.

Name_____   Date_____

Subtract to Get the Target

Directions

- Set the timer. Write in box A as many subtraction equations as you can that equal 0.
- Count how many equations you wrote. Write the number at the bottom of the paper. Check your answers with a calculator. Circle the correct answers and count them. Write the number at the bottom of the paper.
- Set the timer. Repeat the activity for the numbers in boxes B, C, and D.

A. 0	B. 1
C. 5	D. 2

A. I wrote _____ equations.   A. I wrote _____ correct equations.

B. I wrote _____ equations.   B. I wrote _____ correct equations.

C. I wrote _____ equations.   C. I wrote _____ correct equations.

D. I wrote _____ equations.   D. I wrote _____ correct equations.

Name_____   Date_____

Get the Target

Directions

- Set the timer. Write in box A as many <u>addition</u> and <u>subtraction</u> equations as you can that equal 3.
- Count how many equations you wrote. Write the number at the bottom of the paper. Check your answers with a calculator. Circle the correct answers and count them. Write the number at the bottom of the paper.
- Set the timer. Repeat the activity for the numbers in boxes B, C, and D.

A.	3	B.	8
C.	5	D.	4

A. I wrote _____ equations.		A. I wrote _____ correct equations.
B. I wrote _____ equations.		B. I wrote _____ correct equations.
C. I wrote _____ equations.		C. I wrote _____ correct equations.
D. I wrote _____ equations.		D. I wrote _____ correct equations.

Math Fun for Two or More Players

Name_____ Date _____

Double-Digit Target

Directions

- Set the timer. Write in box A as many <u>addition</u> and <u>subtraction</u> equations as you can that equal 11.
- Count how many equations you wrote. Write the number at the bottom of the paper. Check your answers with a calculator. Circle the correct answers and count them. Write the number at the bottom of the paper.
- Set the timer. Repeat the activity for the numbers in boxes B, C, and D.

A. 11	B. 15
C. 20	D. 13

A. I wrote _____ equations.
B. I wrote _____ equations.
C. I wrote _____ equations.
D. I wrote _____ equations.

A. I wrote _____ correct equations.
B. I wrote _____ correct equations.
C. I wrote _____ correct equations.
D. I wrote _____ correct equations.

Use Your Memory

Materials

Levels

1. Addition Memory (page 60)
   ADDITION
2. Subtraction Memory (page 61)
   SUBTRACTION
3. Add and Subtract Memory (page 62)
   ADDITION, SUBTRACTION
4. Multiplication Memory (page 63)
   MULTIPLICATION

✓ reproducibles (choose the appropriate level)
✓ scissors (1 for each group)
✓ resealable plastic bags (1 for each group)

Directions

1. Divide the class into small groups. Give each group a reproducible at the appropriate level, scissors, and a plastic bag (to store cards at the end of their game).

2. Have children cut apart and shuffle the math memory cards. Tell them to place the cards facedown in rows on a flat surface.

3. Have each player, in turn, pick up two cards, read aloud the math problems, and say the answer to each problem. If the two answers are the same, the player keeps the cards. If the answers are different, he or she returns the cards to their original position.

4. Have children continue to play until all cards are removed. The player with the most cards is the winner.

Helpful Hints

➤ Photocopy each Memory reproducible on a different color of construction paper so pieces for different games will not get mixed up with each other.

➤ On the Add and Subtract Memory reproducible (page 62), each addition problem has a subtraction problem as its match (e.g., 3 + 2 and 14 – 9).

Math Fun for Two or More Players

Addition Memory

Directions

- Cut apart the cards. Mix the cards. Place them facedown in rows.
- Pick up two cards. Read the addition problems. Say the sums.
- If the two sums are the same, keep the cards. If the sums are different, return the cards.
- Take turns playing until all of the cards are removed. The player with the most cards is the winner.

9 + 9	8 + 4	6 + 3	5 + 3	7 + 4
4 + 5	6 + 5	9 + 4	3 + 4	10 + 8
7 + 6	9 + 1	5 + 9	8 + 2	8 + 7
6 + 1	9 + 6	4 + 4	9 + 3	7 + 7

Subtraction Memory

Directions

- Cut apart the cards. Mix the cards. Place them facedown in rows.
- Pick up two cards. Read the subtraction problems. Say the differences.
- If the two differences are the same, keep the cards. If the differences are not the same, return the cards.
- Take turns playing until all of the cards are removed. The player with the most cards is the winner.

12 − 10	13 − 4	15 − 9	15 − 8	15 − 5
19 − 7	16 − 8	13 − 8	15 − 3	17 − 6
18 − 7	8 − 1	12 − 7	9 − 5	12 − 4
16 − 6	9 − 7	12 − 8	12 − 3	14 − 8

Math Fun for Two or More Players

Add and Subtract Memory

Directions

- Cut apart the cards. Mix the cards. Place them facedown in rows.
- Pick up two cards. Read the math problems. Say the answers.
- If the two answers are the same, keep the cards. If the answers are different, return the cards.
- Take turns playing until all of the cards are removed. The player with the most cards is the winner.

6 + 8	16 − 10	8 + 8	18 − 8	3 + 1
18 − 6	13 + 4	17 − 9	5 + 7	20 − 3
3 + 5	19 − 3	9 + 9	14 − 9	3 + 7
12 − 8	3 + 2	17 − 3	2 + 4	19 − 1

Multiplication Memory

Directions

- Cut apart the cards. Mix the cards. Place them facedown in rows.
- Pick up two cards. Read the multiplication problems. Say the products.
- If the two products are the same, keep the cards. If the products are different, return the cards.
- Take turns playing until all of the cards are removed. The player with the most cards is the winner.

10 x 1	6 x 2	2 x 1	5 x 4	5 x 8
10 x 4	5 x 0	3 x 5	10 x 5	2 x 6
7 x 2	5 x 6	5 x 2	2 x 7	10 x 3
5 x 10	2 x 0	1 x 2	2 x 10	5 x 3

Math Fun for Two or More Players

Number Duel

Materials

Levels

1. ● 1-Digit Duel (page 65)
   NUMBER COMPARISON OF ONES
2. ● 2-Digit Duel (page 66)
   NUMBER COMPARISON OF TENS
3. ● 3-Digit Duel (page 67)
   NUMBER COMPARISON OF HUNDREDS
4. ● 4-Digit Duel (page 68)
   NUMBER COMPARISON OF THOUSANDS

✔ reproducibles (choose the appropriate level)

✔ **Number Cards** (page 84)

✔ resealable plastic bags (1 for each child)

Directions

1. Photocopy and cut apart a set of Number Cards for each player, and store each set in a separate plastic bag.

2. Divide the class into small groups. Give each child in a group the same reproducible and a bag of cards. Tell players to shuffle their cards and place the cards facedown in front of them.

3. Have players, in turn, choose a card without looking at it and place it in any square until all their squares are filled. (Note: Once cards are placed, they cannot be moved.)

4. Invite each player to read aloud his or her top number and ask *Is this number greater than the other players' top number?* The child with the largest number scores 1 point. (Note: In the event of a tie, both players score 1 point.)

5. Invite each player to read aloud his or her bottom number and ask *Is this number less than the other players' bottom number?* The child with the smallest number scores 1 point.

6. Encourage groups to play until a player scores 10 points.

Helpful Hints

➤ Encourage children to use manipulatives (e.g., crackers) to keep score.

➤ Review greater than, less than, and equal to with children. Discuss place value and how to correctly read numbers.

64 Math Fun for Two or More Players

1-Digit Duel

Directions

- Mix your cards. Place them facedown.
- Take turns choosing a card. Place the card in any square. Fill all your squares.
- Read your top number. Ask yourself *Is this number greater than the other players' top number?* The player with the largest number scores 1 point.
- Read your bottom number. Ask yourself *Is this number less than the other players' bottom number?* The player with the smallest number scores 1 point.
- Play until a player scores 10 points.

Is this number **greater than** the other players' top number?

Is this number **less than** the other players' bottom number?

2-Digit Duel

Directions

- Mix your cards. Place them facedown.
- Take turns choosing a card. Place the card in any square. Fill all your squares.
- Read your top number. Ask yourself *Is this number greater than the other players' top number?* The player with the largest number scores 1 point.
- Read your bottom number. Ask yourself *Is this number less than the other players' bottom number?* The player with the smallest number scores 1 point.
- Play until a player scores 10 points.

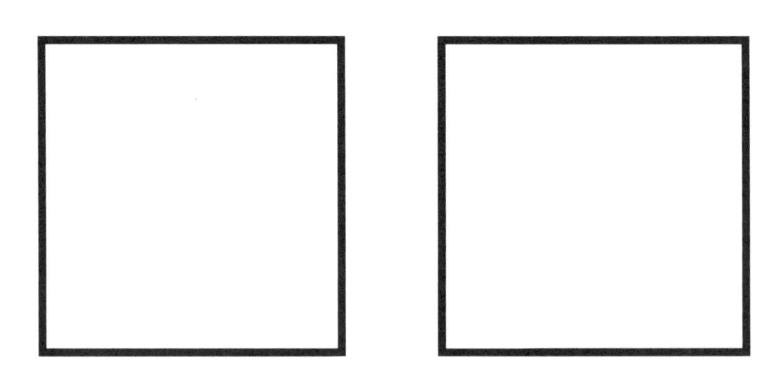

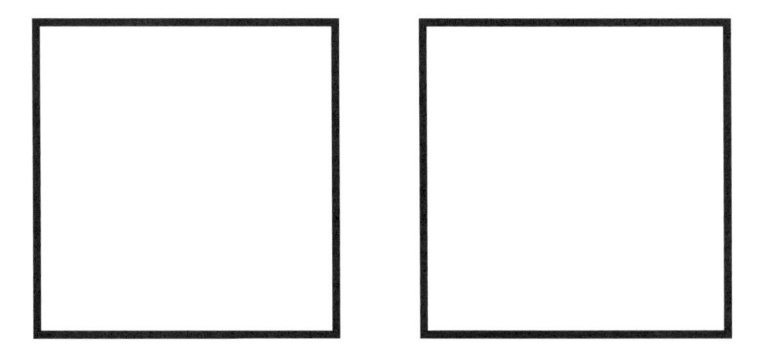

Is this number **greater than** the other players' top number?

Is this number **less than** the other players' bottom number?

3-Digit Duel

Directions

- Mix your cards. Place them facedown.
- Take turns choosing a card. Place the card in any square. Fill all your squares.
- Read your top number. Ask yourself *Is this number greater than the other players' top number?* The player with the largest number scores 1 point.
- Read your bottom number. Ask yourself *Is this number less than the other players' bottom number?* The player with the smallest number scores 1 point.
- Play until a player scores 10 points.

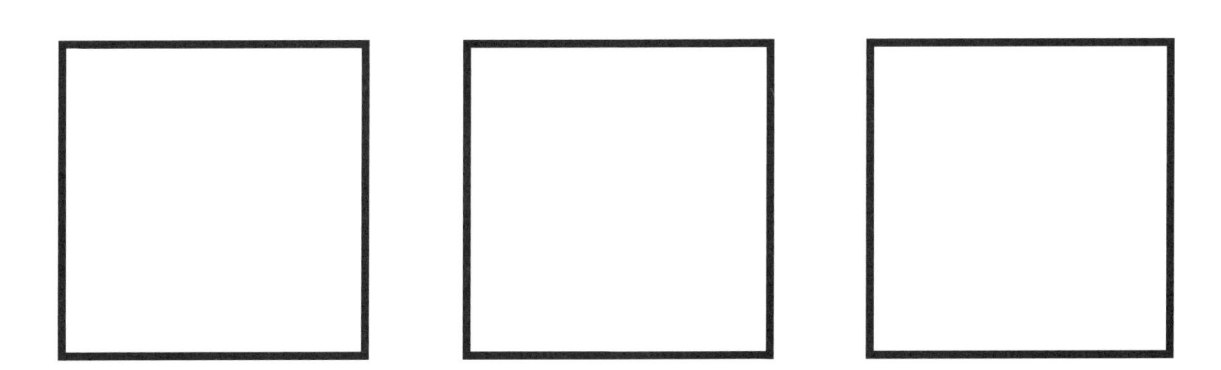

☐ ☐ ☐

Is this number **greater than** the other players' top number?

☐ ☐ ☐

Is this number **less than** the other players' bottom number?

4-Digit Duel

Directions

- Mix your cards. Place them facedown.
- Take turns choosing a card. Place the card in any square. Fill all your squares.
- Read your top number. Ask yourself *Is this number greater than the other players' top number?* The player with the largest number scores 1 point.
- Read your bottom number. Ask yourself *Is this number less than the other players' bottom number?* The player with the smallest number scores 1 point.
- Play until a player scores 10 points.

☐ , ☐ ☐ ☐

Is this number **greater than** the other players' top number?

☐ , ☐ ☐ ☐

Is this number **less than** the other players' bottom number?

68 Math Fun for Two or More Players

Score More

Materials

Levels

- ✓ reproducibles (choose the appropriate level)
  - **1** ● Basketball Score (page 70)
    ADDITION, PROBLEM SOLVING
  - **2** ● Soccer Score (page 71)
    ADDITION, SUBTRACTION, PROBLEM SOLVING
  - **3** ● Baseball Score (page 72)
    ADDITION, SUBTRACTION, PROBLEM SOLVING
  - **4** ● Football Score (page 73)
    ADDITION, SUBTRACTION, MULTIPLICATION, PROBLEM SOLVING
- ✓ **Smile Squares** (page 91)
- ✓ **Spinners** (pages 92–93)
- ✓ resealable plastic bags (1 for each group)

Directions

1. Photocopy a set of Smile Squares and the appropriate spinner for each game board. Cut apart the Smile Squares, assemble the spinner, write *Spinner A* or *B* on the back, and place each set of materials in a bag.

2. Give a group of two or three children a reproducible at the appropriate level and a bag of materials.

3. Have players, in turn, spin their spinner twice; add, subtract, or multiply (depending on the game) the two numbers; and cover their answer with a Smile Square. (Note: No number can be covered twice.)

4. Explain that players score 1 point for each already covered circle on their group's game board that is connected to the circle they just covered.

5. Tell players that if they spin and are unable to cover a number, they lose their turn. If a number *could* have been covered, any player can cover the space and score points.

6. When a player cannot cover a number in three successive turns, he or she is out of the game. The game ends when all players are out or when all numbers are covered. The player with the most points is the winner.

Helpful Hints

- ➤ Give a multiplication table to children using the Football Score reproducible.

- ➤ Instead of Spinner A, you can use a pair of dice for Basketball Score, Soccer Score, and Football Score.

- ➤ Invite children to play a variation of the game in which they only score 1 point if the connected circle is covered by an opponent's Smile Square. (Photocopy Smile Squares on different colored paper to distinguish players' pieces.)

Basketball Score

Directions

- Spin Spinner A twice. Add the two numbers. Find the sum on the game board. Cover it with a Smile Square.
- You score 1 point for each covered circle that is connected to the circle you covered.
- If you cannot cover a number, you lose your turn. If a number *could* have been covered, any player can cover it and score points.
- You are out of the game when you cannot cover a number for three turns in a row. The game ends when all players are out or when all of the numbers are covered. The player with the most points is the winner.

70 Math Fun for Two or More Players

Soccer Score

Directions

- Spin Spinner A twice. Add or subtract the two numbers (e.g., 4 + 3 = 7 or 4 − 3 = 1). Find the answer on the game board. Cover it with a Smile Square.

- You score 1 point for each covered circle that is connected to the circle you covered.

- If you cannot cover a number, you lose your turn. If a number *could* have been covered, any player can cover it and score points.

- You are out of the game when you cannot cover a number for three turns in a row. The game ends when all players are out or when all of the numbers are covered. The player with the most points is the winner.

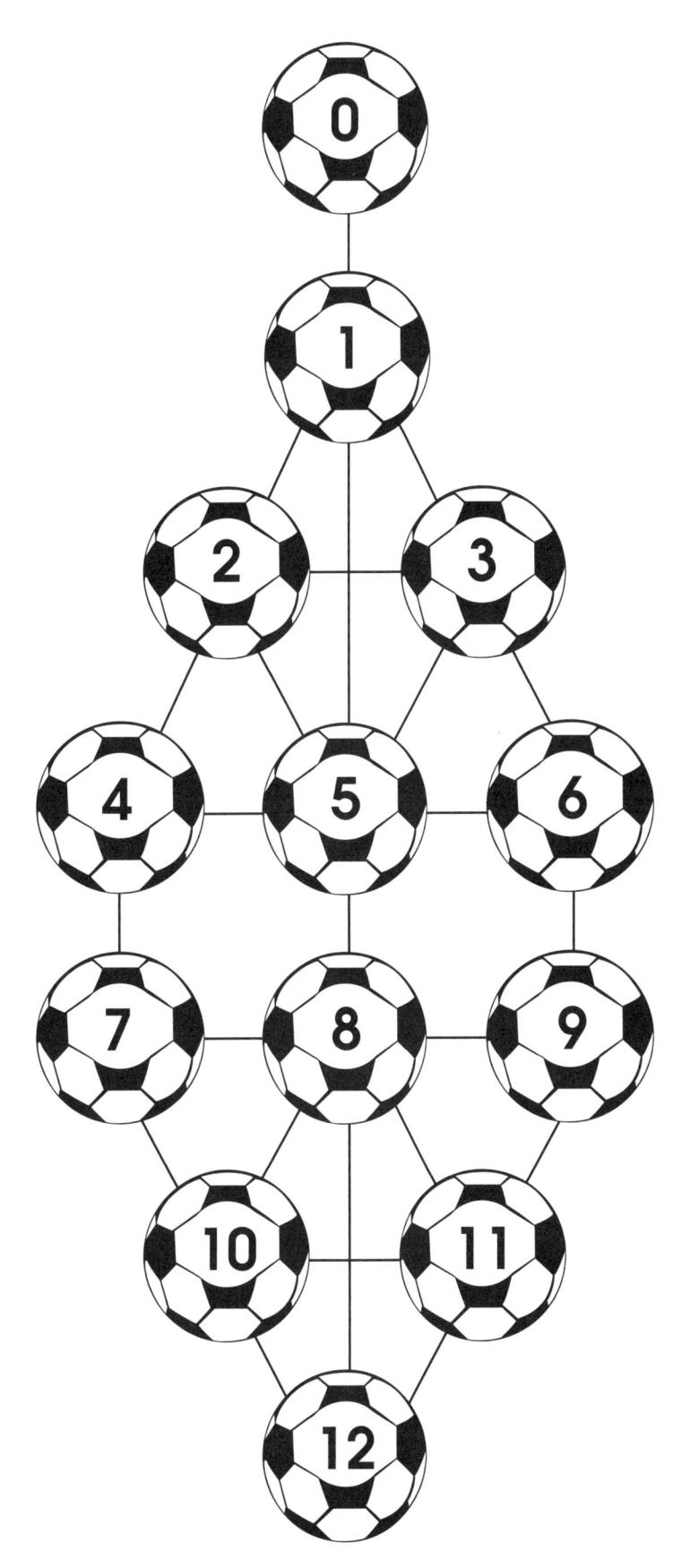

Baseball Score

Directions

- Spin Spinner B twice. Add or subtract the two numbers (e.g., 4 + 3 = 7 or 4 – 3 = 1). Find the answer on the game board. Cover it with a Smile Square. (You can cover more than one circle with the same number in it.)
- You score 1 point for each covered circle that is connected to the circle you covered.
- If you cannot cover a number, you lose your turn. If a number *could* have been covered, any player can cover it and score points.
- You are out of the game when you cannot cover a number for three turns in a row. The game ends when all players are out or when all of the numbers are covered. The player with the most points is the winner.

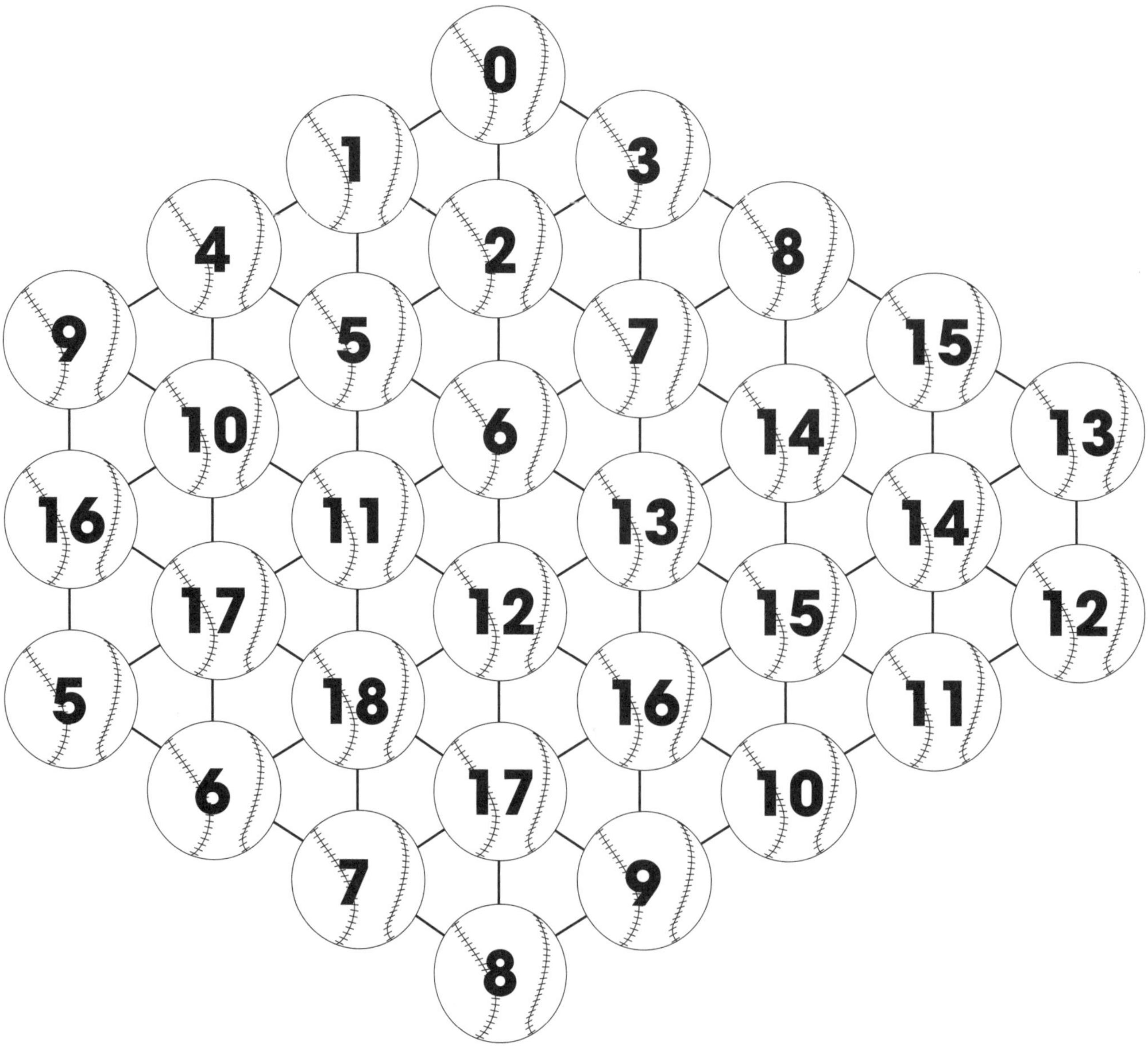
0
1
3
4
2
8
9
5
7
15
10
6
14
13
16
11
13
14
17
12
15
12
5
18
16
11
6
17
10
7
9
8

Football Score

Directions

- Spin Spinner A twice. Add, subtract, or multiply the two numbers (e.g., 4 + 3 = 7 or 4 − 3 = 1 or 4 x 3 = 12). Find the answer on the game board. Cover it with a Smile Square
- You score 1 point for each covered circle that is connected to the circle you covered.
- If you cannot cover a number, you lose your turn. If a number *could* have been covered, any player can cover it and score points.
- You are out of the game when you cannot cover a number for three turns in a row. The game ends when all players are out or when all of the numbers are covered. The player with the most points is the winner.

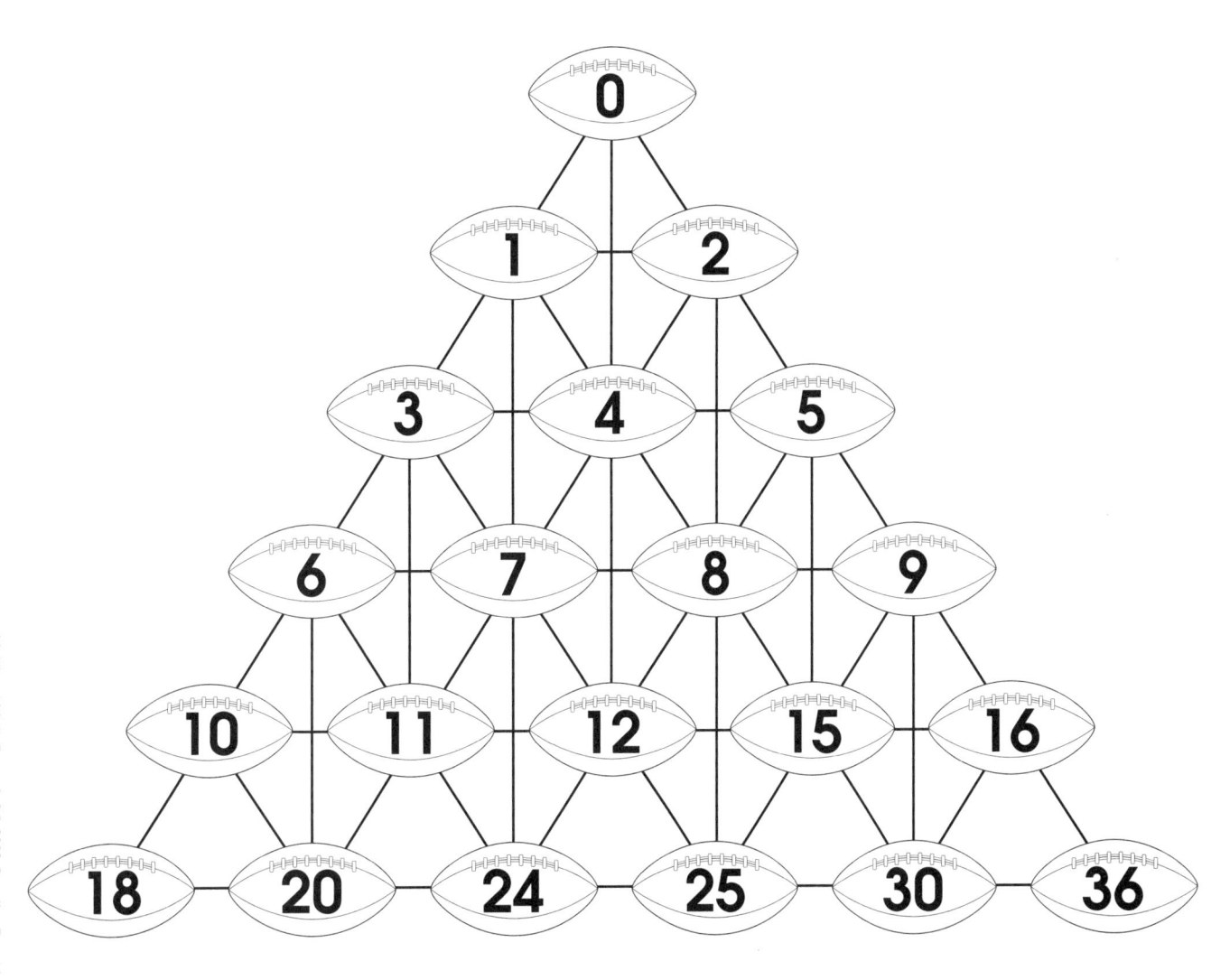

```
                    0
                 1     2
              3     4     5
           6     7     8     9
       10    11    12    15    16
    18    20    24    25    30    36
```

Math Fun for Two or More Players

Spin the Wheel

Materials

Levels

- ✓ reproducibles (choose the appropriate level)
  - ① Spin to 10 (page 75)
    ADDITION, PROBLEM SOLVING, ALGEBRA
  - ② Spin to 18 (page 76)
    ADDITION, PROBLEM SOLVING, ALGEBRA
  - ③ Spin to 20 (page 77)
    ADDITION, REGROUPING, PROBLEM SOLVING, ALGEBRA
  - ④ Spin to 30 (page 78)
    ADDITION, REGROUPING, PROBLEM SOLVING, ALGEBRA
- ✓ Spinner B (page 93)
- ✓ scratch paper

Directions

1. Divide the class into small groups. Give each group a spinner, and give each child in a group the same reproducible and scratch paper.

2. Tell players that the object of the game is to write numbers in the circles so each line equals the target sum. (Explain that some of their lines will not equal the target sum and that they will not receive points for these lines.)

3. Have players, in turn, spin and write the number landed on in any circle. (Note: Numbers cannot be moved later.) Tell players that they can reject any four numbers by writing them in the hexagons. Encourage players to add the numbers in each line on scratch paper.

4. Explain that players score 1 point for each correct equation they complete. The player with the most points is the winner.

Helpful Hints

➢ Invite players to use a calculator to check their equations.

➢ Have children play a variation of this game in which they cannot repeat the same number in an equation (e.g., 5 + 5 = 10 would not be allowed).

➢ Add challenge to the game at any level. Give each child two sets of Number Cards (page 84) instead of Spinner B. Have children place their cards facedown in front of them and choose a card on each turn.

74 Math Fun for Two or More Players

Name_____   Date_____

Spin to 10

Directions

- Try to make each line add up to 10.
- Take turns. Spin the spinner. Write the number in any circle. Reject any four numbers by writing them in the hexagons.
- The game ends when all players complete their paper. You score 1 point for each correct equation you complete. The player with the most points is the winner.

◯ + ◯ = 10

◯ + ◯ = 10

◯ + ◯ = 10

◯ + ◯ = 10

◯ + ◯ = 10

Rejects

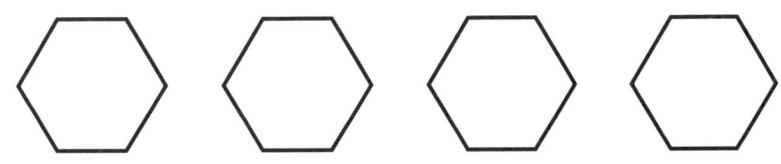

⬡ ⬡ ⬡ ⬡

Points: _____

Math Fun for Two or More Players

Spin to 18

Directions

- Try to make each line add up to 18.
- Take turns. Spin the spinner. Write the number in any circle. Reject any four numbers by writing them in the hexagons.
- The game ends when all players complete their paper. You score 1 point for each correct equation you complete. The player with the most points is the winner.

◯ + ◯ + ◯ = 18

◯ + ◯ + ◯ = 18

◯ + ◯ + ◯ = 18

◯ + ◯ + ◯ = 18

◯ + ◯ + ◯ = 18

Rejects

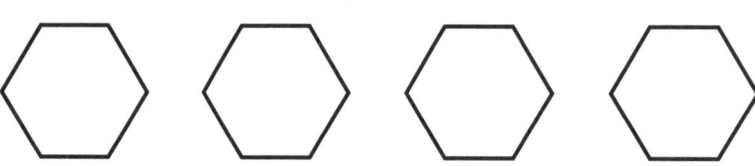

⬡ ⬡ ⬡ ⬡

Points: _____

Name_____ Date _____

Spin to 20

Directions

- Try to make each line add up to 20.
- Take turns. Spin the spinner. Write the number in any circle. Reject any four numbers by writing them in the hexagons.
- The game ends when all players complete their paper. You score 1 point for each correct equation you complete. The player with the most points is the winner.

◯ + ◯ + ◯ + ◯ = 20

◯ + ◯ + ◯ + ◯ = 20

◯ + ◯ + ◯ + ◯ = 20

◯ + ◯ + ◯ + ◯ = 20

◯ + ◯ + ◯ + ◯ = 20

Rejects

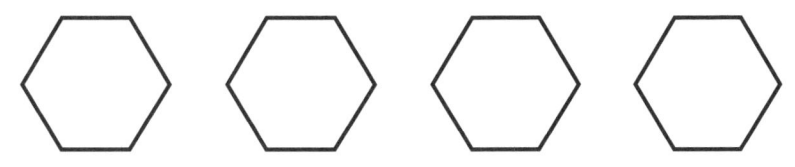

⬡ ⬡ ⬡ ⬡

Points: _____

Name_____   Date_____

Spin to 30

Directions

- Try to make each line add up to 30.
- Take turns. Spin the spinner. Write the number in any circle. Reject any four numbers by writing them in the hexagons.
- The game ends when all players complete their paper. You score 1 point for each correct equation you complete. The player with the most points is the winner.

◯ + ◯ + ◯ + ◯ + ◯ = 30

◯ + ◯ + ◯ + ◯ + ◯ = 30

◯ + ◯ + ◯ + ◯ + ◯ = 30

◯ + ◯ + ◯ + ◯ + ◯ = 30

◯ + ◯ + ◯ + ◯ + ◯ = 30

Rejects

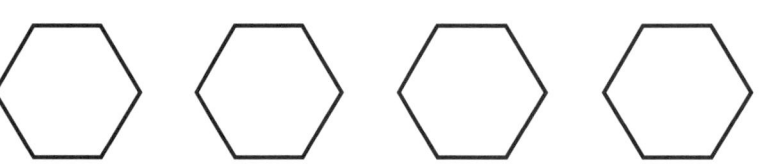

⬡ ⬡ ⬡ ⬡

Points: _____

78 Math Fun for Two or More Players

Math Flash Cards

2	two
1	one
0	zero

Math Flash Cards

5	five
4	four
3	three

80 Manipulatives and Game Pieces

Math Flash Cards

8	eight
7	seven
6	six

Manipulatives and Game Pieces 81

Math Flash Cards

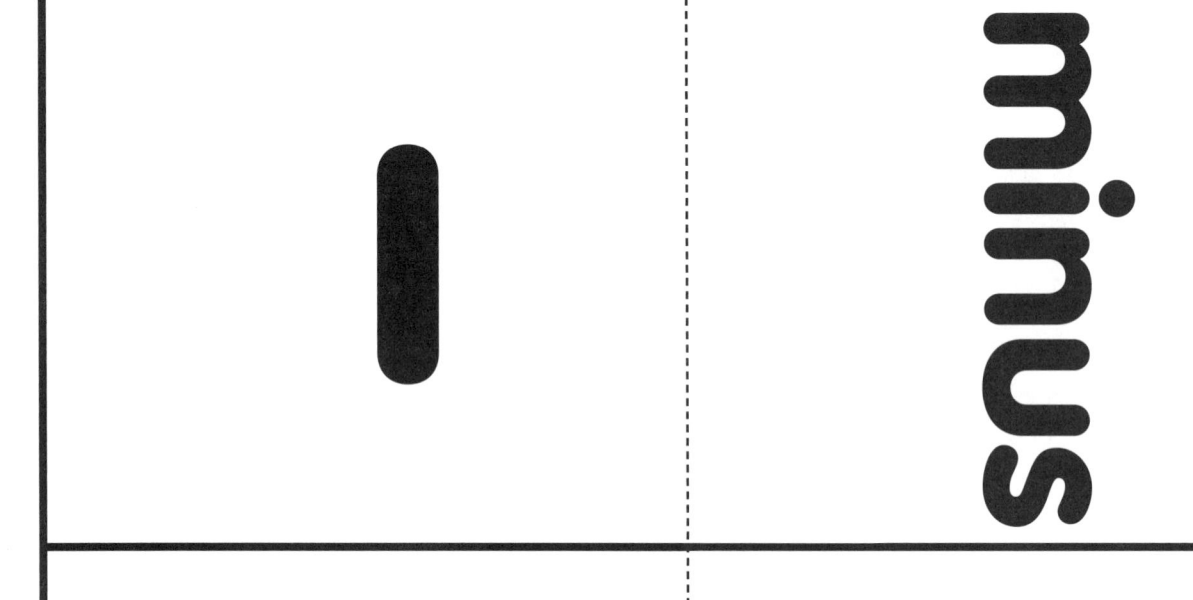

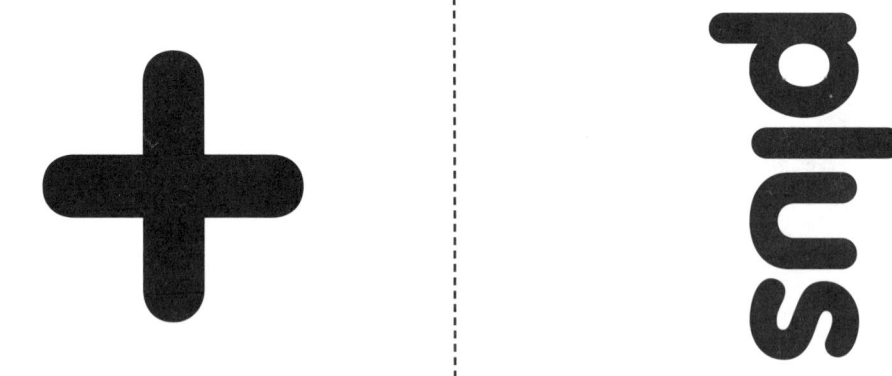

—	minus
+	plus
9	nine

Math Flash Cards

>	greater than
<	less than
=	equals

Number Cards

Use with
- The In-Between Game (pages 38–42)
- Watch for the Answer (pages 48–51)
- Number Duel (pages 64–68)

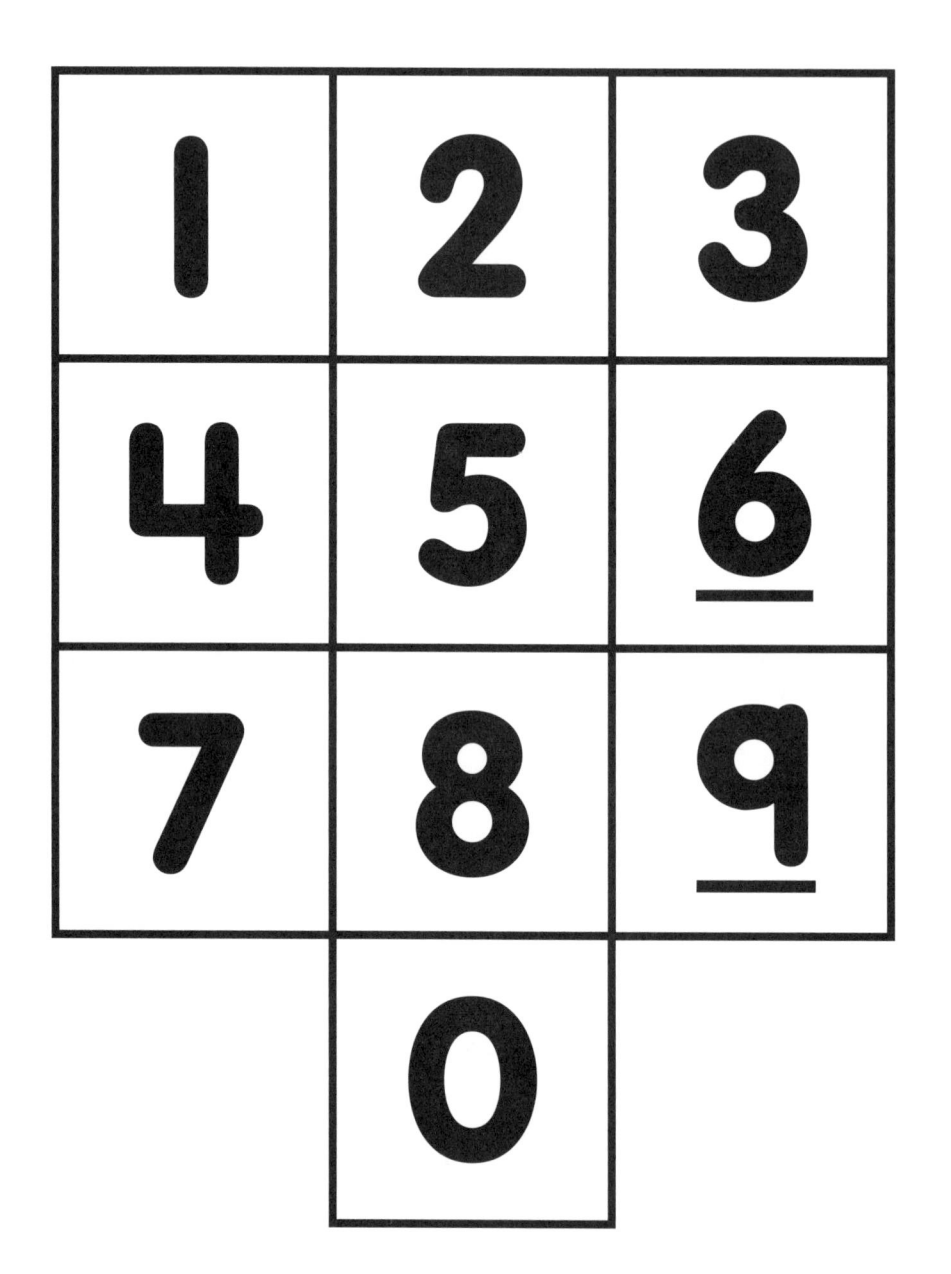

1	2	3
4	5	6
7	8	9
	0	

Fraction Cards

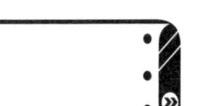

Set A

Use with
- Bear Fraction Board (page 44)
- Toucan Fraction Board (page 45)

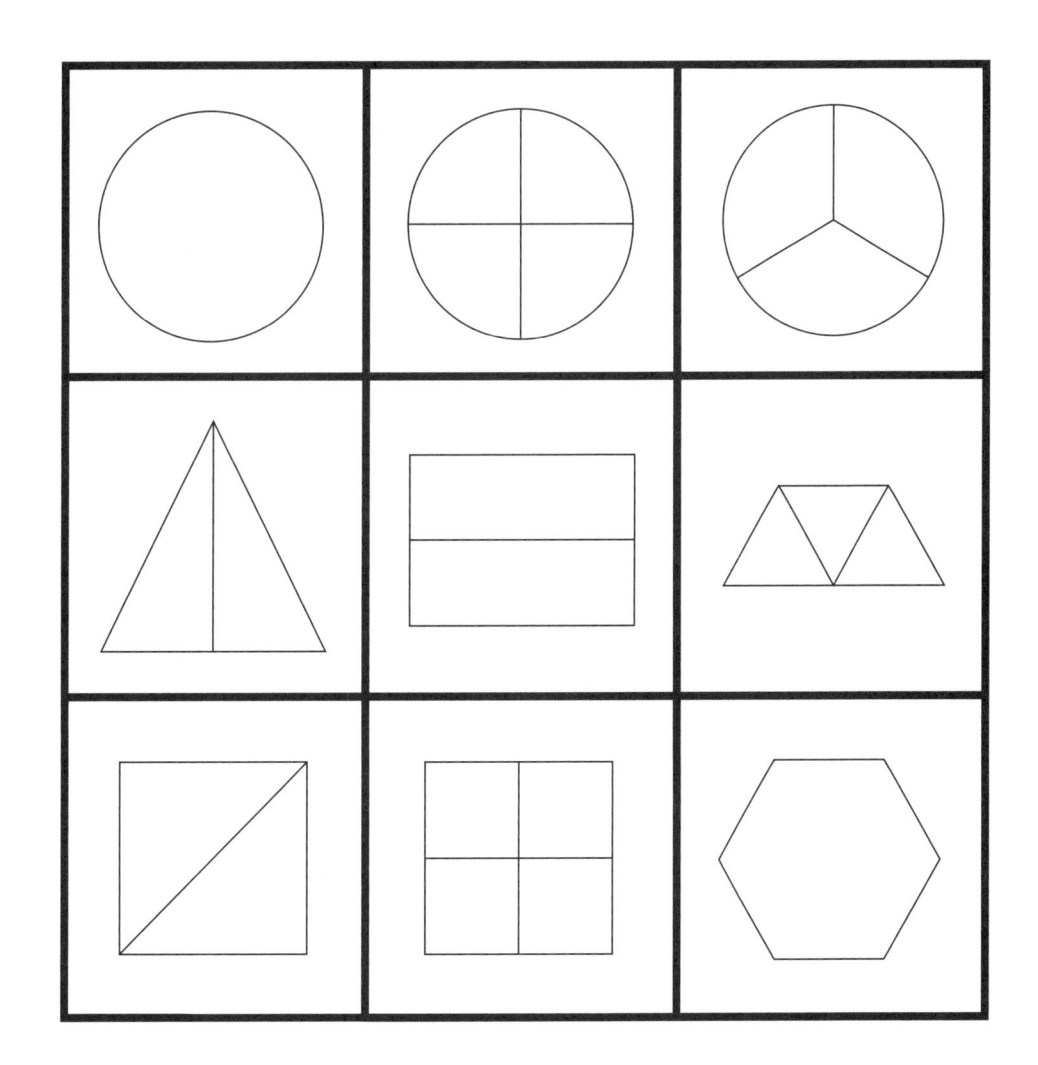

Fraction Cards

Set B

Use with
- Snake Fraction Board (page 46)
- Octopus Fraction Board (page 47)

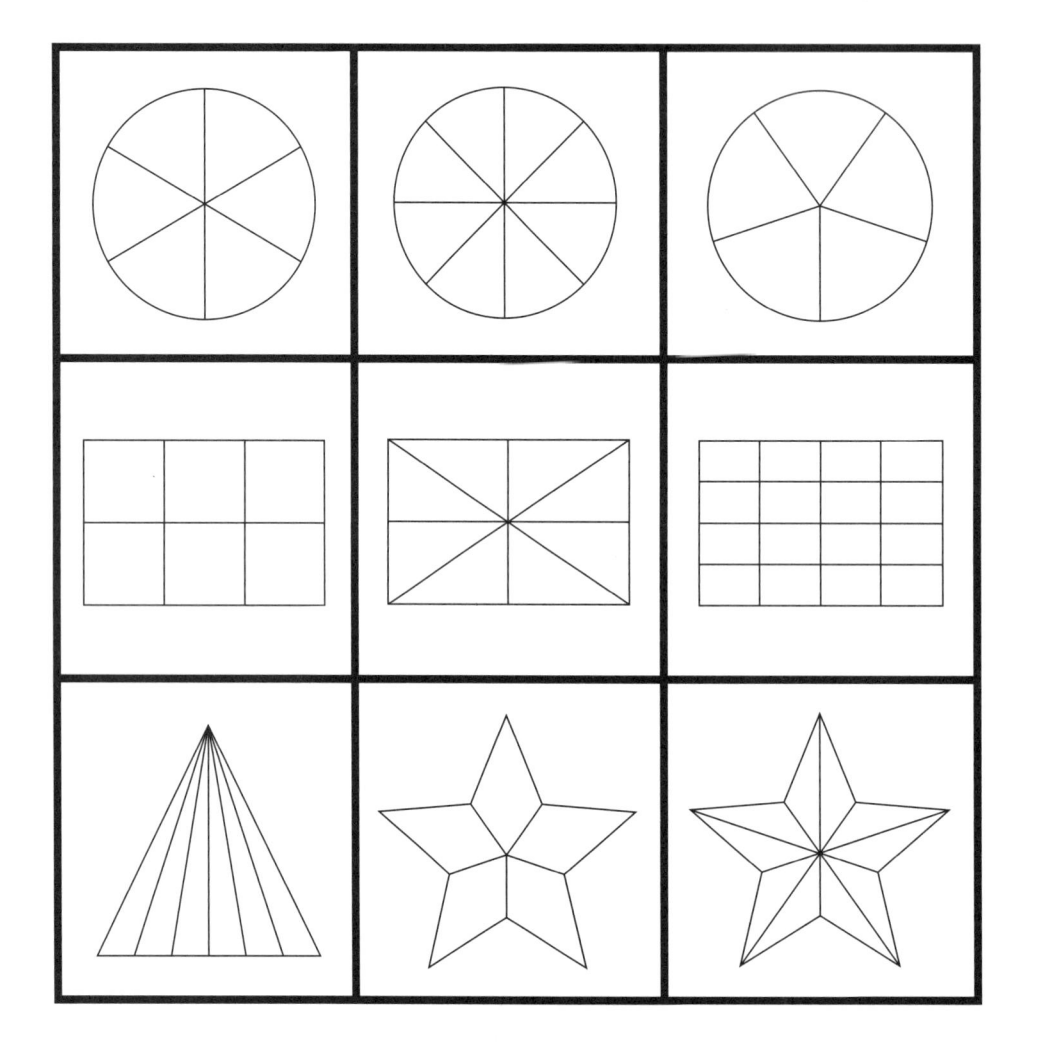

Hour Clocks

Use with
- Earlier or Later? (pages 52–53)

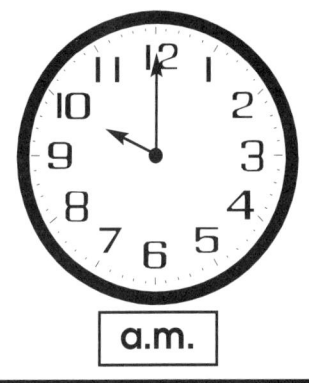

a.m.	p.m.
p.m.	a.m.
a.m.	p.m.
p.m.	a.m.

Manipulatives and Game Pieces 87

Half-Hour Clocks

Use with
- Earlier or Later? (pages 52–53)

a.m.	p.m.
p.m.	a.m.
p.m.	a.m.
p.m.	p.m.

88 Manipulatives and Game Pieces

Quarter-Hour Clocks

Use with
- Earlier or Later? (pages 52–53)

a.m.	p.m.
p.m.	p.m.
p.m.	p.m.
p.m.	a.m.

Manipulatives and Game Pieces 89

5-Minute Clocks

Use with
- Earlier or Later? (pages 52–53)

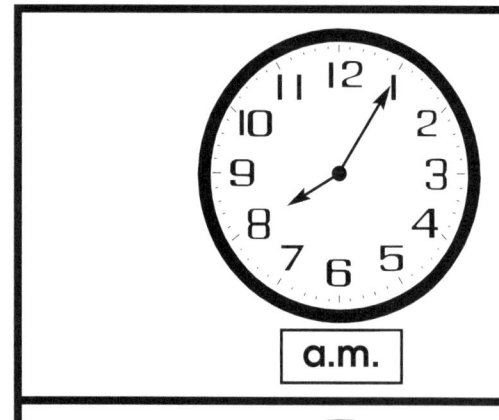

a.m.	p.m.
a.m.	a.m.
p.m.	p.m.
a.m.	p.m.

Smile Squares

Use with
- Score More (pages 69–73)

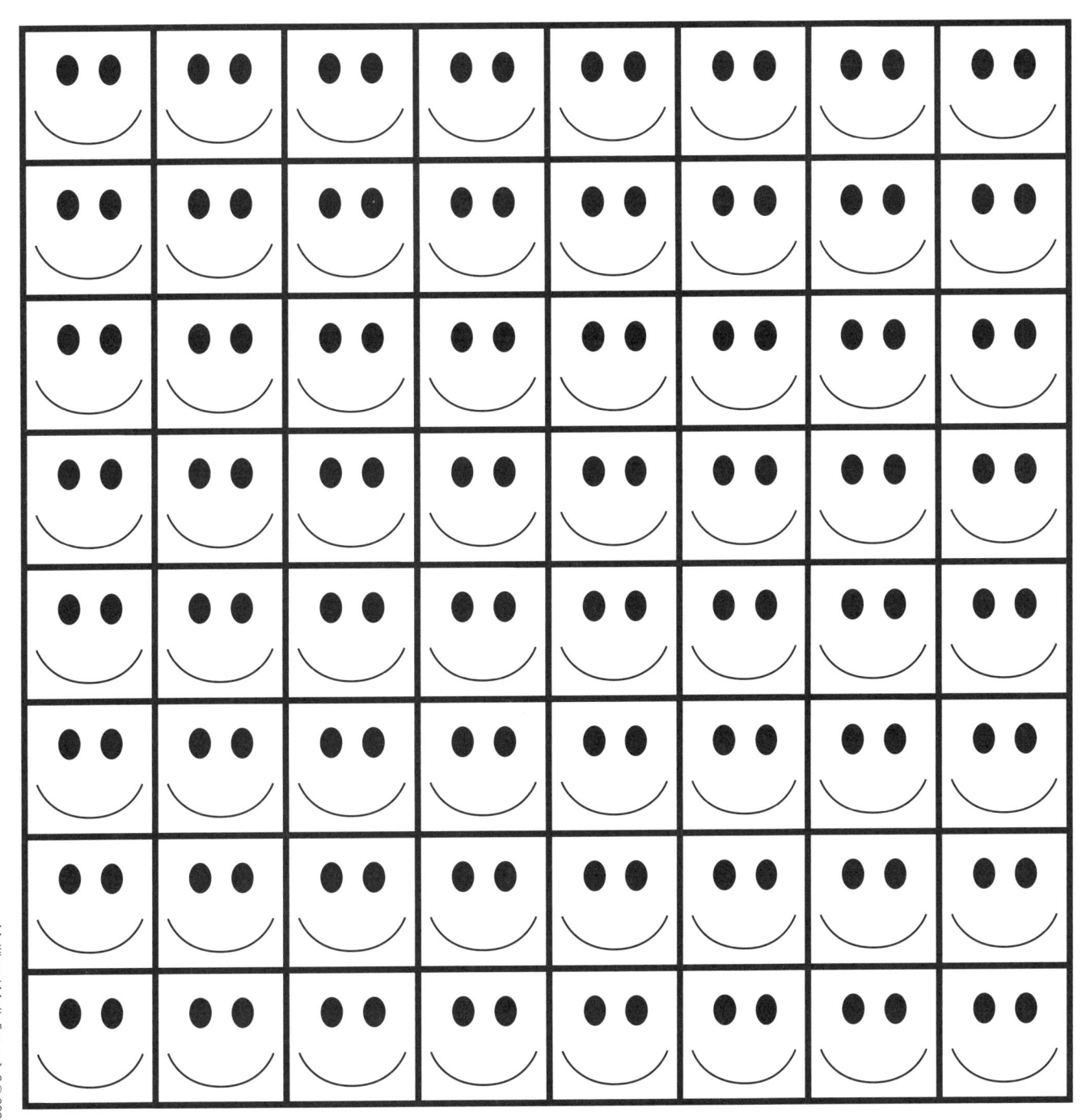

Photocopy the Smile Squares on card stock, and then cut them apart. Store each set of squares in a plastic bag.

Spinner A

Use with
- Basketball Score (page 70)
- Soccer Score (page 71)
- Football Score (page 73)

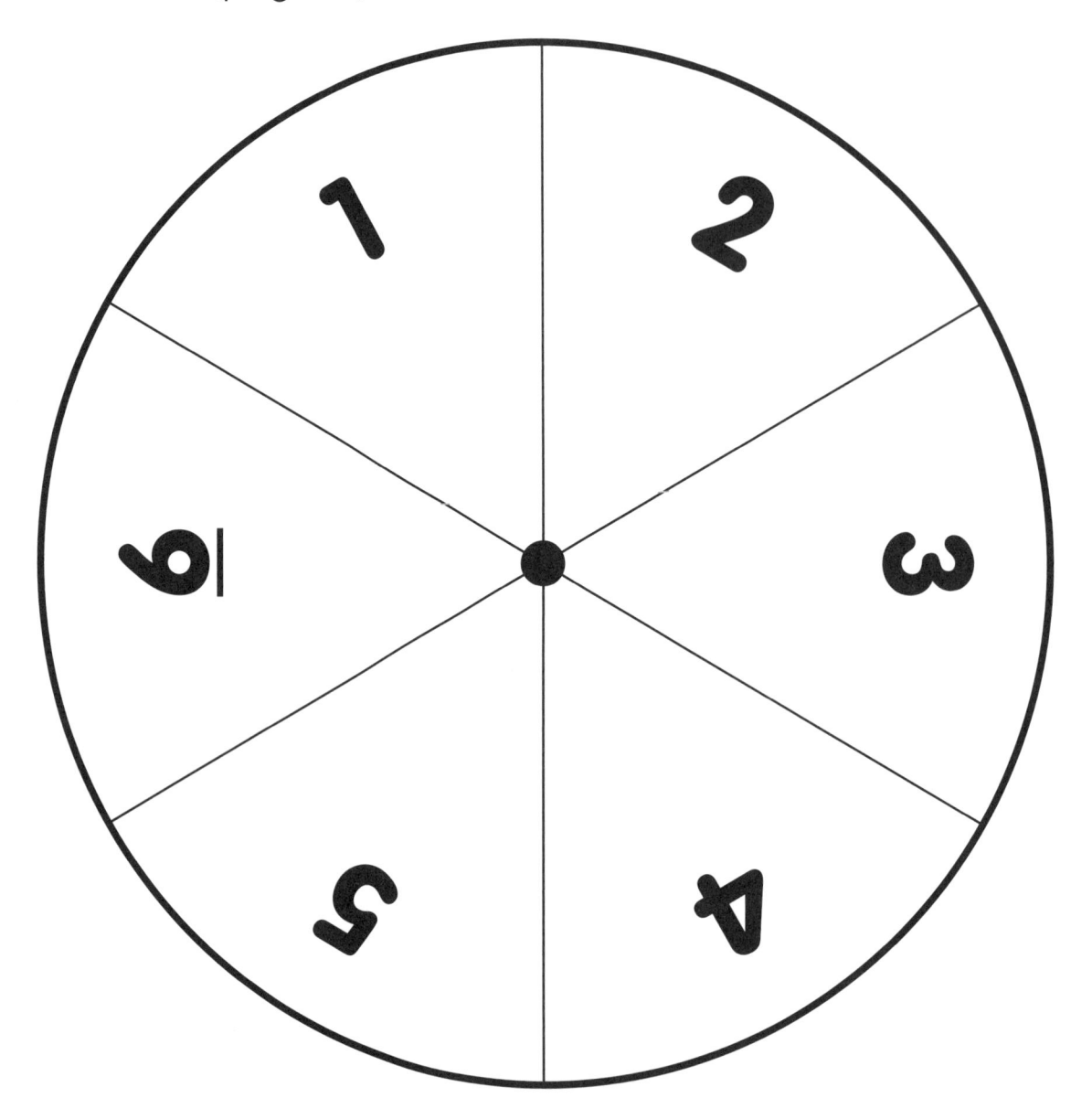

Photocopy on card stock, laminate, and cut out the spinner. Write *Spinner A* on the back. Put a brass fastener through the end of a paper clip, and push the fastener through the center of the spinner. (Option: Place the end of a paper clip over the center circle on the spinner. Put a pencil point inside the paper clip on the center circle. Hold the pencil firmly, and spin the paper clip.)

Spinner B

Use with
- Baseball Score (page 72)
- Spin the Wheel (pages 74–78)

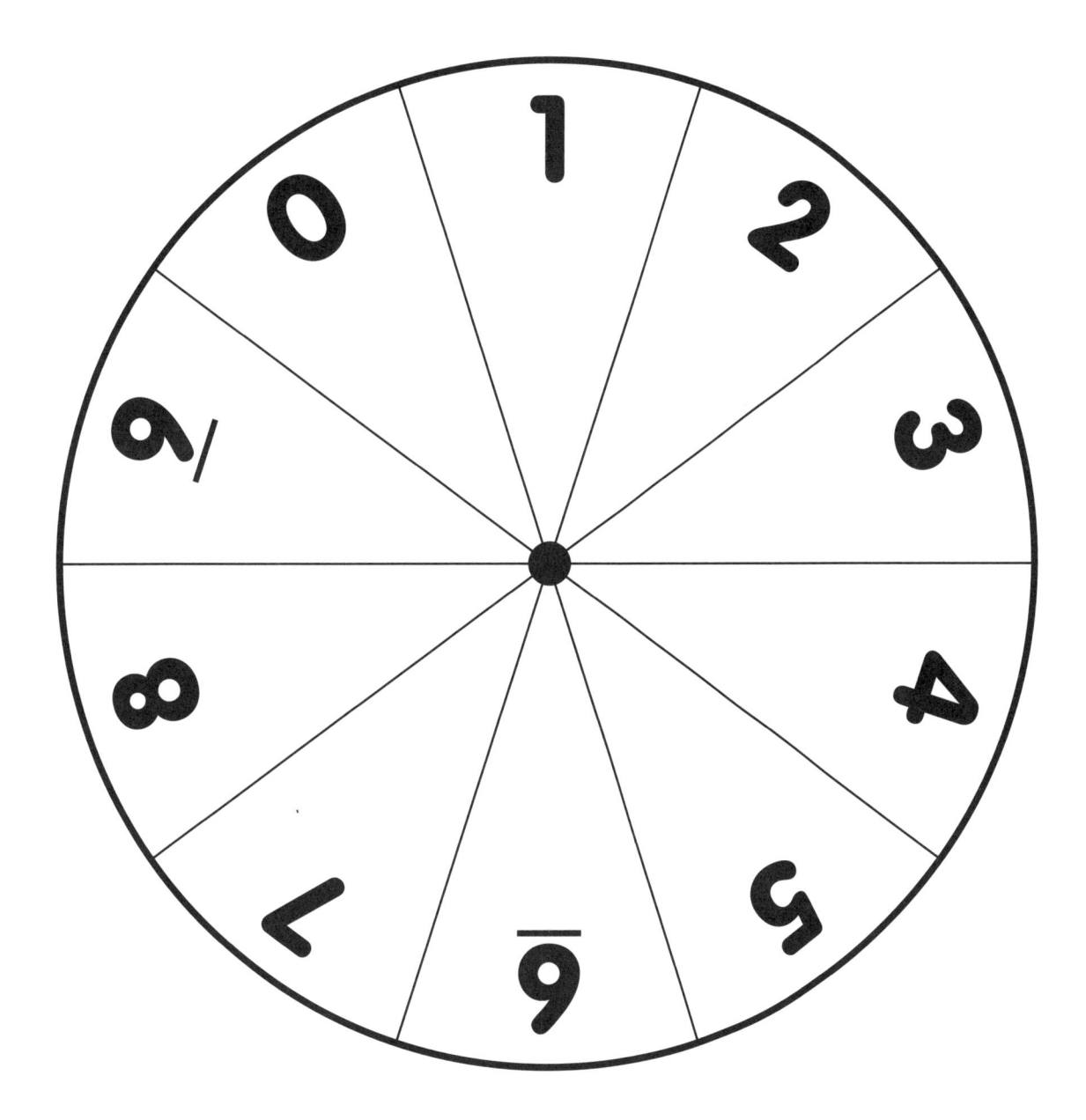

Photocopy on card stock, laminate, and cut out the spinner. Write *Spinner B* on the back. Put a brass fastener through the end of a paper clip, and push the fastener through the center of the spinner. (Option: Place the end of a paper clip over the center circle on the spinner. Put a pencil point inside the paper clip on the center circle. Hold the pencil firmly, and spin the paper clip.)

Manipulatives and Game Pieces 93

Answers

Page 14

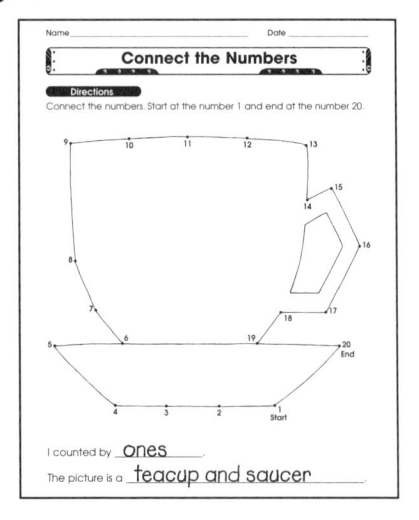

Connect the Numbers

I counted by __ones__.
The picture is a __teacup and saucer__.

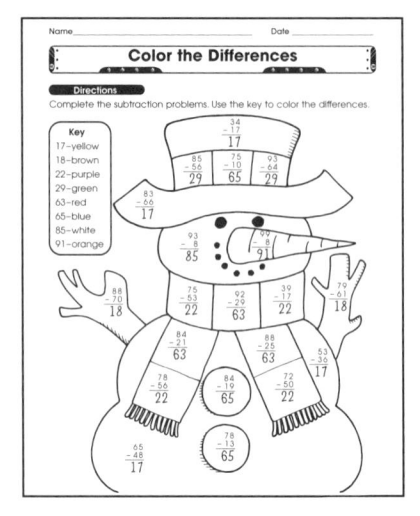

Page 15

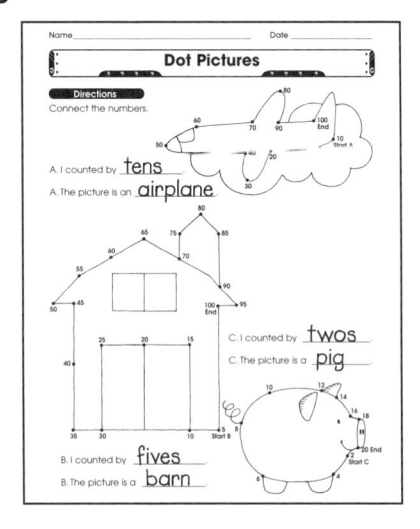

Dot Pictures

A. I counted by __tens__.
A. The picture is an __airplane__.

B. I counted by __fives__.
B. The picture is a __barn__.

C. I counted by __twos__.
C. The picture is a __pig__.

Page 16

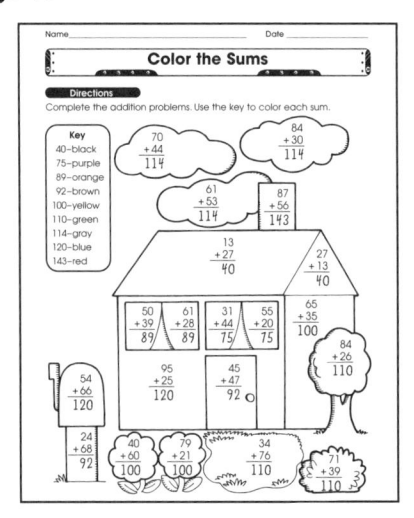

Color the Sums

Page 17

Color the Differences

Page 19

Hidden Numbers

I found __4__ hidden zeros.
I found __2__ hidden threes.
I found __5__ hidden fives.
I found __3__ hidden eights.
I found __5__ hidden nines.

Page 20

Flat Shape Find

A □ is called a __rectangle__. I found __2__ of them.
A ▢ is called a __square__. I found __6__ of them.
A ○ is called a __circle__. I found __4__ of them.
A ⬡ is called a __hexagon__. I found __1__ of them.
A △ is called a __triangle__. I found __7__ of them.

94 Answers

Answers

Page 21

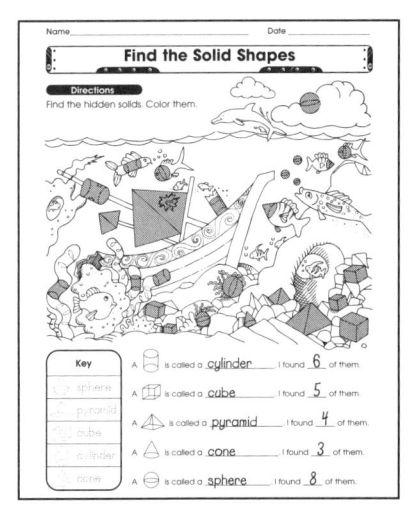

Find the Solid Shapes

A cylinder — I found 6 of them.
A cube — I found 5 of them.
A pyramid — I found 4 of them.
A cone — I found 3 of them.
A sphere — I found 8 of them.

Page 22

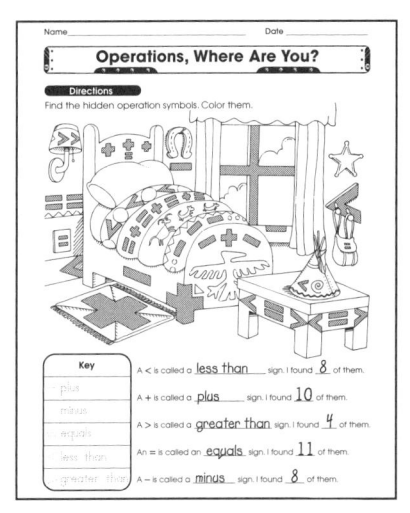

Operations, Where Are You?

A < is called a less than sign. I found 8 of them.
A + is called a plus sign. I found 10 of them.
A > is called a greater than sign. I found 4 of them.
An = is called an equals sign. I found 11 of them.
A − is called a minus sign. I found 8 of them.

Page 24

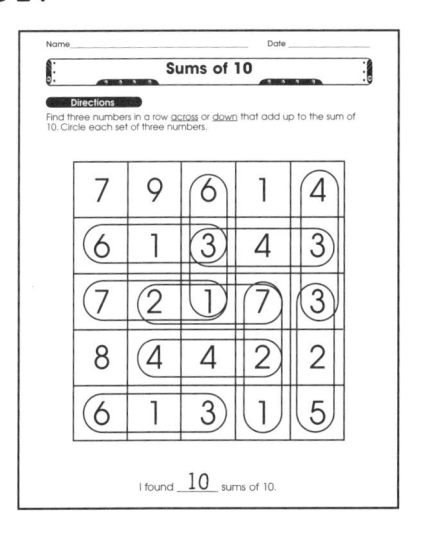

Sums of 10

I found 10 sums of 10.

Page 25

Sums of 12

I found 15 sums of 12.

Page 26

Sums of 20

I found 16 sums of 20.

Page 27

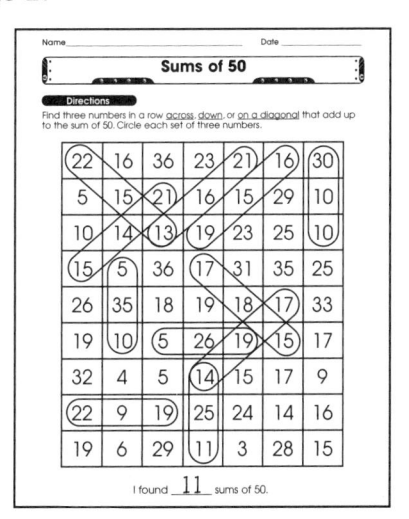

Sums of 50

I found 11 sums of 50.

Answers

Page 29

24

Page 30

2

Page 31

8

Page 32

14

Page 34

Bird's Path to 10

The path of numbers that adds up to 10 is
2 + 5 + 0 + 1 + 0 + 2 = 10

Page 35

Spider's Path to 5

The path of numbers that when subtracted equals 5 is
18 − 3 − 0 − 1 − 4 − 2 − 1 − 2 = 5

Page 36

Monkey's Path to 40

The path of numbers that adds up to 40 is
3 + 9 + 1 + 2 + 3 + 5 + 0 + 3 + 7 + 6 + 0 + 1 = 40

Page 37

Snail's Path to 15

The path of numbers that when subtracted equals 15 is
68 − 4 − 13 − 1 − 0 − 2 − 4 − 10 − 3 − 4 − 2 − 0 − 1 − 8 − 1 = 15

96 Answers